praise for

"This is the book we've been waiting for! Bringing together some of the most brilliant minds and courageous voices in the world—from university scholars to grassroots activists, political organizers to political prisoners—Smiley uses the power of dialogue to help us teach, dream, plan, and struggle toward an abolitionist future. Read *Defund* and prepare to be challenged, educated, and inspired."

—MUMIA ABU-JAMAL, coeditor of
Beneath the Mountain: An Anti-Prison Reader

"*Defund* is a rich and valuable contribution to the abolitionist canon. Through impressively wide-ranging and refreshingly radical conversations, Smiley and his comrades dare us to bravely imagine a world beyond prisons, policing, and other state-sanctioned systems of violence, repression, and exploitation. They also provide us with the practical tools and actionable strategies necessary to bring such a world into existence."

—MARC LAMONT HILL, author of
We Still Here: Pandemic, Policing, Protest, and Possibility

"These conversations offer us an opportunity to interrogate the promise and process of defunding the police from a variety of perspectives. A new world is possible, but this volume reminds us that we have a lot of thinking and organizing to do to achieve it."

—ALEX S. VITALE, author of *The End of Policing*

"Enacting deep conversation and abolitionist imagination, *Defund* exemplifies the centrality of dynamic study to the ongoing work of radical collectives, organizations, and movements. Smiley builds on his scholarly activist experience to catalyze dialogue with a group of abolition practitioners who understand that the defund mandate 'does not refer to *some* police but rather *all* police.' This book makes a vital contribution to post-2020 abolitionist debates around state power, autonomous infrastructure, and insurgent futurity."

—DYLAN RODRÍGUEZ, author of the Frantz Fanon Award–winning
White Reconstruction: Domestic Warfare and the Logics of Genocide

"This deeply engaging book puts scholars, activists, and criminal justice survivors in conversation with Calvin John Smiley as together they explore the possibilities of defunding and disempowering state violence. The book's collaborative structure models the very dynamic needed for confronting the prison and the police: an interplay of inclusive, community-based movements working along a continuum from reformist defunding to radical abolition. In this battle, Smiley argues for hope; his book delivers it."

—JEFF FERRELL, author of *Drift: Illicit Mobility and Uncertain Knowledge*

"The discussions in *Defund* are provocative and inspiring. Smiley, in dialogue with other abolitionist scholar/activists, presents a vision of a collaborative, caring future where harm reduction and life-affirming communities are possible."

—LORI GRUEN, professor of philosophy, Wesleyan University, and coeditor of *Carceral Logics: Human Incarceration and Animal Captivity*

"Once again, Smiley tackles a complex topic fraught with racism in our criminal legal system and unpacks it with flawless writing and a bright light. Defunding the police is often misunderstood and simplified. *Defund* offers the most insightful explanation of what it means and how it intersects with class, poverty, cultural stereotypes, incarceration, abolition, and colonialism, particularly colonial capitalism. In addition to detailing the terrific historical events that brought us to the #Defund movement, Smiley's interviews are astute and gripping. Despite the resistance to the #Defund movement (and even idea), Smiley provides examples of concrete and often successful inspirational activism in the face of major opposition. This is a must-read for criminologists and would be a great book to assign to students."

—JOANNE BELKNAP, professor emerita of ethnic studies, University of Colorado–Boulder, and past president and fellow of the American Society of Criminology

defund

conversations
toward abolition

CALVIN JOHN SMILEY

Haymarket Books
Chicago, IL

Published in 2024 by
Haymarket Books
P.O. Box 180165
Chicago, IL 60618
773-583-7884
www.haymarketbooks.org
info@haymarketbooks.org

ISBN: 979-8-88890-096-3

Distributed to the trade in the US through Consortium Book Sales and Distribution (www.cbsd.com) and internationally through Ingram Publisher Services International (www.ingramcontent.com).

This book was published with the generous support of Lannan Foundation, Wallace Action Fund, and the Marguerite Casey Foundation.

Special discounts are available for bulk purchases by organizations and institutions. Please email info@haymarketbooks.org for more information.

Cover and book design by Jamie Kerry.

Printed in Canada by union labor.

Library of Congress Cataloging-in-Publication data is available.

10 9 8 7 6 5 4 3 2 1

For the youth who have, and will, pass through Horizon and Crossroads Juvenile Centers because of nothing more than the zip codes where they were born. The opportunity to work with you continues to inspire my abolitionist dream for facilities like this to cease to exist.

"Until he free, I'm raisin' hell"

—Pop Smoke, "Dior" (Summer 2020 Protest Anthem)

Contents

Graffiti on the side of a building in Brooklyn, New York, June 4, 2022. Photo by Calvin John Smiley.

The Defund Mo(ve)ment

I n fall 2021, I taught my first course in person since the onset of the COVID-19 global pandemic in March 2020. The City University of New York (CUNY) required that students and staff be vaccinated, wear protective coverings, and practice social distancing within indoor spaces. My class, entitled Criminal Justice and Public Policy, introduces students to policy-related issues that govern the criminal legal system, including an examination of the history of punishment; policing, courts, and corrections; reentry; reform; and abolition.

Still on the heels of the summer 2020 uprisings in the wake of the murder of George Floyd by police officers in Minnesota, the killing of Breonna Taylor in a "botched" no-knock raid carried out by cops in Kentucky, and the filmed lynching of Ahmaud Arbery by White supremacist vigilantes in Georgia,[1] students were eager to discuss policy implications because they perceived the gravity of the mass global protests in response to these deaths, law enforcement counter-responses to these rebellions, and the subsequent aftermaths, including the call for defund.

During the semester, we deliberated on various local issues related to New York City's criminal legal system. Notably, outside of New York, students were closely monitoring a ballot initiative in Minnesota that sponsored the dismantling of the Minneapolis Police Department. This policy proposal was a direct response to the death of George Floyd and the summer 2020 movements that utilized defund to envision abolitionist possibilities.

Led by the Black Visions Collective's Yes 4 Minneapolis campaign, the purpose of this vote was to unequivocally eliminate police from the city and replace this institution with a new department of public safety, which would incorporate peace officers to promote safety and public health.[2] The abolition of formal police officers was imagined as the first step in reinvesting in the community and developing innovative strategies for neighborhood efficacy through implementing safeguards and care for neighborhoods at the local level.

Unfortunately, city residents rejected the Yes 4 Minneapolis campaign, and the metropolis retained their police department.[3] Despite the failure of the ballot initiative, these efforts brought awareness to the history of the Minneapolis police disproportionately brutalizing and harassing Black residents, like many police agencies around the United States. According to the *New York Times*, "African-Americans account for about 20 percent of [Minneapolis's] population, but they are more likely to be pulled over, arrested and have force used against them than white residents, Police Department data shows. And black people accounted for more than 60 percent of the victims in Minneapolis police shootings from late 2009 through May 2019, data shows."[4] Beyond the murder of George Floyd, Minneapolis police killed several other residents in recent years, including Justine Ruszczyk in 2017, Thurman Blevins in 2018, and Chiasher Fong Vue in 2019.[5] This aligned with a Department of Justice report that found disproportionate and systemic discrimination against Black residents, who were arrested and fined at higher rates than their White counterparts.[6] Northwestern University professor Keeanga-Yamahtta Taylor describes this as "literally extorting the Black population," as local municipalities subsidize their budgets with these fines and fees via the criminal legal system.[7] Finally, in June 2023, the Department of Justice released a report investigating Minneapolis and their police department finding, "systemic problems in MPD [Minneapolis Police Department] made what happened to George Floyd possible."[8]

The week after the November 2021 election results, my students and I discussed the rejection of the ballot initiative to eliminate the Minneapolis police. Numerous students expressed a sense of defeat; several of them were active participants in CUNY for Abolition and Safety, an anti-racist student coalition formed to pressure CUNY to divest from prisons and policing, and to invest in Black students' well-being and safety.[9] Amid the ensuing discussion, a White male student suggested this vote revealed that "abolition was too extreme." A self-described progressive, this student was not intentionally presenting a case of "told you so" but rather a pessimism to which many living in the American capitalist system default. He queried: "Can you describe any situation where there are no police?"

In that moment, I reminded the class of the arguments presented in two abolitionist texts: *Are Prisons Obsolete?* and *Abolition Democracy*,[10] both by Angela Y. Davis. In each of these books, the celebrated scholar-activist highlights that prisons, and by extension police, are not naturally occurring entities in our world. Indeed, both institutions were invented and therefore can also be dismantled.

The class meeting ended in what felt like an impasse. Nevertheless, I attempted to model optimism for those feeling hopeless in that instant, indicating that the mere fact of this vote's occurrence showed how far the defund movement had come in a short period of time. And while the ballot initiative did not pass, folks were now increasingly thinking outside of conventional norms and structures. In sum, it was on account of defund that abolition was being considered.

Days later, I revisited organizer and educator Mariame Kaba's book *We Do This 'Til We Free Us*, and was reminded of her often-cited phrase "Hope is a discipline."[11] In an interview with Kim Wilson and Brian Sonsenstein for their *Beyond Prisons* podcast, Kaba remarks, "Hope doesn't preclude feeling sadness or frustration or anger or any other emotion that makes total sense."[12] In a world that can often feel overwhelming, these are sobering words. I, like my students, had hoped for the vote in Minneapolis to be the cascading breakthrough. Yet, it was not. During the same election cycle, in November 2021, New York elected the second Black mayor in the city's history. Eric Adams, a Republican turned Democrat, had run on a campaign emphasizing his experience as a former police officer, situating himself as the expert on all things "crime." This win, especially given the progressive field of candidates against which Adams ran, sowed doubt as to whether defund had run its course.

In the face of such disorientation, Kaba's words serve as an important reminder: "Hope is a discipline . . . and we have to practice it every single day."[13] Her exhortation is a guiding light for a struggle for liberation that endures many shortcomings, pitfalls, and potential missteps along the road—none of which can be allowed to deter our collective movement(s) from forging ahead, forming alliances, recruiting accomplices, and protecting ourselves.

Crucially, Kaba observes that this struggle will endure beyond our lifetimes: "I take a long view . . . I'm definitely not going to be even close to around for seeing the end of it."[14] The reality is that it took centuries to build and design these systems that we are actively attempting to navigate, untangle, and dismantle. It would be naive to believe these systems will fall overnight; rather, we must constantly remember the long-term visions that will sustain movements, building off previous legacies as we learn to correct and shift our strategies in the face of new challenges. Hope is a discipline that incorporates love, appreciation, kindness, understanding, forgiveness, grief, and anger. Ultimately, we need to make space for these things to happen—whether independently or all at once—as well as be able to feel different things at different moments, unapologetically, at varying stages of the struggle to defund the police, prisons, and systems of injustice.

Through pointed interviews with scholars, activists, and justice-impacted individuals, this book situates the summer 2020 uprisings in the context of ongoing struggles against White supremacist capitalist hegemony, state-sanctioned police violence, and mass incarceration. In particular, the conversations that follow interrogate the rise of the defund mo(ve)ment[15] as both slogan and praxis, and the role of defund in bridging the divide between reform and abolition by working through these ideological tensions.

Ultimately, defund is a moment within a broader movement. First, it is important to define defund. For some, it is about the reallocation of public funds away from police and other punitive carceral systems such as jails, prisons, and surveillance technology and into social welfare programs that provide care, stability, and community. Here, defund is simply a pragmatic and programmatic public policy shift of resources, which is within the power of elected officials and lawmakers.

For others, defund is part of a larger legacy of struggles for racial justice, gender equality, and working-class power. Often, movements are decried for not achieving their goals immediately. Yet, social movement theory highlights that these campaigns take time to build out platforms, identities, grievances, goals, and tasks.[16] For example, the US civil rights movement of the mid-twentieth century, which sought to eradicate legalized racial segregation, discrimination, and disenfranchisement, is often portrayed as an overnight success led by Dr. Martin Luther King Jr. However, this is simply not true. Indeed, a decade of struggle separated the 1954 Supreme Court ruling on *Brown v. Board of Education*, which found racial discrimination in schools to be unconstitutional, and the passage of the 1964 Civil Rights Act. During that period, individuals and organizations strategized, debated, and implemented a range of tactics, including nonviolent direct action, boycotts, and mass marches to garner attention, awareness, and pressure on elected officials to make policy changes. Furthermore, while liberal and progressive commentators, politicians, and educators triumphalize the achievements of the civil rights movement, many of the problems it sought to rectify persist today.[17] Therefore, defund needs time to grow, flourish, and continue to expand on its initial premise as a divest/reinvest strategy, which is to simply move funds from one area that creates harm and into other initiatives that align with care.

Second, we must recognize the salience of defund as a watchword, both within and outside the United States,[18] that captures an entire movement. To that end, we have seen how mainstream political parties have responded. On the one hand, many Democrat leaders and politicians have attempted to distance themselves from the phrase, downplaying its relevancy and hoping it goes away. For example, President Joe Biden has repeatedly argued against defund, saying in his 2022 State of the Union address, "We should all agree the answer is not to defund the police. It's to fund the police. Fund them. Fund them."[19] Furthermore, Democratic congresswoman Cori Bush has been criticized by colleagues for her support of defund. In response to such criticism, Bush stated:

> I always tell [fellow Democrats], "If you all had fixed this before I got here, I wouldn't have to say these things." ... Defund the police is not the problem. . . . We dangled the carrot in front of people's faces and said we can get it done and that Democrats deliver, when we haven't totally delivered.[20]

Bush emphasizes the urgent need for accountability, highlighting that her party cannot rely on rhetoric as a platform but must act in the face of the extraordinary danger the police present—especially to communities that look like the constituents that she represents.

On the other hand, Republican leaders, positioning themselves as the party of "law and order" and "back the blue,"[21] have appropriated the phrase when it suits their political agenda. For example, Republican congresswoman Marjorie Taylor Greene tweeted #DefundTheFBI in response to the law enforcement agency's raid of former President Donald Trump's Florida home.[22] Trump, too, has used the phrase, writing on his Truth Social platform, "Republicans in Congress should defund the DOJ and FBI until they come to their senses."[23] In a moment of rising fascism and anti-intellectualism among the GOP—emblematized by the party's efforts to ban books, prohibit access to gender-affirming care, and pass legislation that revokes the teaching of topics broadly labeled "critical race theory"—Republicans understand the power of this phrase to evoke their base and conjure dissent.

Finally, defund is uniquely positioned to bring reformists and abolitionists together. While the former strategize to perfect the system that is in place and the latter organize to dismantle that system, each can find relevancy in defund. For reformers, defund is a budget issue. In sum, reformers can pressure public officials to shift money into other areas of the public sector to broaden the social safety net. This can be done through sustained petitioning, advocacy, and voting to replace elected officials with leaders who recognize the foundational necessity of a strong welfare state to improve the lives of residents. Conversely, defund appeals to abolitionists because it is the impetus for the eradication of systems of exploitation and violence. Abolitionists can envision defund as a pathway for removing funds from punitive and carceral systems to the point that they are no longer relevant or needed—and eventually eliminated. Abolitionists understand that voting is only one of a myriad of strategies to create social change. Therefore, abolitionists can utilize these reallocated funds to build infrastructure that does not rely on carceral logics to respond to community harm but rather supports alternative pathways to accountability by affirming care, safety, and justice through restorative and transformative paradigms.

Ultimately, defund gives us a platform and pathway to reimagine a society with less police, more care, and services that meet the needs of all. This book is a tool to think through and discuss how defund goes from a hashtag to a movement to a reality.

FROM #BLM TO #DEFUND

For most of American history, police violence has gone unchecked. Sociologist Alex Vitale, in his seminal book *The End of Policing*, articulates the history of police in the United States as the evolution of a force whose aim is to protect property and control those deemed a threat, such as Irish immigrants in the North and enslaved Africans in the South.[24] Therefore, the origins of policing were founded in a racialized, class-based vision of who is "good" and "bad" that continues to shape modern law enforcement strategies. Further, "copaganda" promotes supportive and positive imagery of police and law enforcement agencies that, in turn, undermine efforts to criticize or change these institutions.[25]

Historically, law enforcement has wielded a monopoly of power over residents through police reports, which are used as the official accounts of events and incidents, despite inconsistencies and corresponding calls for independent oversight. Ida B. Wells, an indomitable investigative journalist and Black feminist, said it best: "Those who commit the murders write the reports."[26] However, the advancement and proliferation of surveillance technology, smart devices, and social media has disrupted the legacy of copaganda. Beginning in the early 2010s, audio and visual objectivity,[27] as well as the use of social media applications to discuss police killings, caused the names of the slain victims to go viral, placing pressure on public officials to investigate these deaths.

Following the killing of seventeen-year-old Trayvon Martin in 2012, #BlackLivesMatter (#BLM) began trending on social media. Soon, more hashtags appeared, including #HandsUpDontShoot, #ICantBreath, and #SayHerName, the latter highlighting disparities in the harms and violence that women of color, gender-nonconforming people, and trans folks experience.[28] Yet, summer 2020 became a culminating moment in this longer movement as "#defund" gained popularity amongst activists across the globe who participated in various demonstrations ranging from London to Seoul and Rio to Nairobi—all challenging police brutality.[29]

Moreover, protesters worldwide recognized the historical and colonial connections of racism and White supremacist hegemony to modern-day capitalism. For instance, in Bristol, activists toppled the statue of Sir Edward Colston, a prominent figure in the Royal African Company, which held the British monopoly over the transatlantic slave trade in the seventeenth century.[30] In Brussels, a statue of King Leopold II, responsible for the murder of tens of millions of Congolese people, was defaced.[31] In Puerto Rico, residents reaffirmed claims of sovereignty and recognized the genocide of the Indigenous Taino people by European explorers.[32] In New York City, the NYPD were charged with protecting a statue of Christopher Columbus, as activists scrawled "Fuck Columbus" along the foundation.[33] In fact, according to Erin L. Thompson, a leading scholar of art crime, at least 170 public monuments in the United States alone were either removed or toppled during the year following the summer 2020 protests.[34]

That summer, #defund replaced #BLM as the rallying cry for the movement, deepening the connections organizers were already drawing between economic exploitation and policing, and underscoring the reality that this structural, racialized, state-sanctioned violence goes far beyond individual instances of brutality. While much of #BLM advocated and championed reforms to policing, setting its sights on justice within American courts and the imprisonment of law enforcement perpetrators, #defund took a bolder step to question the legitimacy, relevancy, and need of policing, the courts, and prisons. In the process, new dialogues and discussions emerged regarding movement-building, coalitions, and strategy.

DEFUND TO ABOLITION

Within abolitionist spaces, defund is not a new concept. Terms such as "decarcerate," "dismantle," and "divest" have all been used to broadly discuss the eradication of systems of repression. However, "defund" as a phrase and tool captured the essence of generations of organizing. Unlike other terms and theories, which can be elusive or abstract, defund pragmatically positions itself as an economic shift away from carceral logics and toward commitments to care.

As stated above, defund calls for economic and social justice by demanding the reallocation of money and resources away from police and other punitive entities, and into other areas of the community such as housing, health care, and education. At root, defund is not a radical idea but a pragmatic one, championing the dream that lies that at the heart of Black Lives Matter: a world where Black lives have the resources they need to flourish. Defund becomes the vehicle to make this happen by operating as a road map for policymakers and elected officials to shift money away from bloated police and carceral budgets and into under-resourced sectors of society, which in turn can create jobs and opportunities with these funds as well as invest in infrastructure that protects everyone.

The COVID-19 global pandemic, which wreaked havoc across the globe, has become a demonstrable argument for defund and toward abolition. Despite the floundering leadership of Donald Trump, the pandemic exposed a dilapidated infrastructure and lack of investment in communities—specifically, the low-income communities of color ravaged by the virus. CUNY Graduate Center presidential professor Marc Lamont Hill describes this as "corona capitalism": a set of economic conditions and institutional arrangements that made the vulnerable more likely to experience premature death during the pandemic.[35] However, at the same time that so many of the vulnerable were left to die, the public encountered, with stark clarity, the viability of a welfare state previously dismissed as pure fantasy as the pandemic forced the government to place moratoriums and freezes on economic burdens such as rent, evictions, and college loan payments. Additionally, a vaccination program was deployed to inoculate all residents, regardless of citizenship status, and provided residents with three stimulus payments to individuals and families. Finally, the Coronavirus Aid, Relief, and Economic Security (CARES) Act helped release individuals in the federal prison system to alleviate the spread of the virus. Some states followed suit, such as New Jersey, which released more than 2,500 people from prison during the peak of the pandemic.[36]

However incomplete and insufficient the COVID-19 response by local, state, and federal authorities, it cast new light on the reality: abolition futures are possible. Government can subsidize housing, provide medical care for all, and decarcerate its prisons. During this time, the country did not implode—and, one cringes to note, some billionaires extended their wealth during the peak of the pandemic, relying on what journalist and activist Naomi Klein calls "disaster capitalism," which highlights how private companies can profit during times of hardship.[37]

The abolitionist movement, which stems from the legacy of the eradication of institutionalized slavery, is finding its footing in the modern era. Since summer 2020, numerous books, including this one, have been published that unpack, think through, and envision abolitionist praxis.[38] Ultimately, I argue, defund continues these generative conversations by becoming a catalyst toward abolitionist visions.

DEFUND FOR THE FUTURE

Defund extends to areas where BLM might falter. For example, as philosopher Olúfémi O. Táíwò argues in his book *Elite Capture: How the Powerful Took Over Identity Politics*, elites have adopted a tactic of performative symbolic identity politics "to pacify protestors without enacting material reforms; and their efforts to rebrand (not replace) existing institutions."[39] In other words, corporate virtue signaling through public relation media campaigns define the boundaries of "acceptable" liberal discourse, distinguishing between more radical calls for defund and cooptation of BLM. For example, mega-corporations like Amazon, one of the most valuable brands in the world, posted "Black lives matter" on their homepage in the wake of George Floyd's murder. Ironically, the organization has deep ties to policing and surveillance technologies that would suggest that Black lives *don't* matter to the company.[40] This example shows how a business that can disregard the lives of its workers and communities across the globe can still post "BLM" without consequence but would not upload defund in the same way, because the interpretation of the latter cannot be co-opted. Further, Princeton professor of African American Studies, Naomi Murakawa articulates how elites have responded to defund by, "repression through a politics of recognition," to usurp movement-building by championing certain reformists positions that reinforce support for carceral logics rather than dismantling them.[41]

To frame my approach to the defund mo(ve)ment, and to abolitionism as a fundamentally futural undertaking, it is worth retracing the roots of my relationship to this work. First, as a sociologist, I think, study, examine, read, and interpret complex social problems, particularly surrounding the concept of carcerality. My training and research inform my belief in abolition. While reforms, particularly non-reformist reforms,[42] as ways to create immediate gains without strengthening the capitalist carceral system, are important steps, if we want a reimagined society, we cannot stop short of anything less than abolitionist visions. Second, and perhaps more importantly, I come to abolition through my activist and advocacy work. I have organized against capital punishment in Pennsylvania, reentry work in New Jersey, and restorative justice with incarcerated youth in New York. Nowhere have prisons worked; rather, I have witnessed the harm incarceration does to society, and this experience has only bolstered my dedication to dismantling vestiges of violence. Abolition is not simply a scholastic exercise, fad, or social experiment; it is a life choice to commit to solidarity, resistance, and subversion of the carceral apparatus at every turn. "Defund the police" does not refer to *some* police but rather *all* police.

Finally, abolition is not a monologue. Therefore, each chapter of this book takes the form of a dialogue. In these generative discussions, scholars, activists, and justice-impacted individuals share their knowledge, expertise, and experiences. I am forever grateful to them, both for accepting my invitation to take part in this project as well as for entrusting me with their words. This stylistic approach builds on Haymarket Books' rich history of publications organized around conversations.[43]

All interviews for this book took place between December 2021 and March 2022 via remote conference call. The decision to adopt this format was not only pragmatic, allowing flexibility across time and location, but also necessary to continue safe social distancing during the pandemic. Each interview has been edited for clarity and succinctness. Because this process involved their labor, all participants were compensated for their time, unless they declined—in which case the honorarium was donated to organizations working to dismantle the carceral state.

Each chapter begins with an introduction of the person(s) interviewed and an overview of our discussion. I hope readers walk away with either a new perspective and appreciation for the defund movement or, at the very least, an understanding of why defund is important to the broader legacy of radical social movements, reimagined justice, a call to action, and commitments to abolitionist futures.

CHAPTER 1

"Policing as a Colonial Project" with Marisol LeBrón

D r. Marisol LeBrón is an associate professor in feminist studies and critical race and ethnic studies at the University of California, Santa Cruz. She has written extensively on policing, social inequality, violence, and protest within Latinx communities, particularly in Puerto Rico.[44] Our conversation revolves around three main issues: colonial capitalism's fundamental dependence on policing, the stakes of protest against such colonial violence, and the challenges abolition must overcome to succeed as a decolonial praxis.

We begin our discussion by unpacking terms such as "colonial capitalism,"—a compound that highlights the geographic dimension of exploitation and profit motive across the past several centuries, from preindustrial times to present. Further, colonial capitalism utilizes law enforcement strategically to ensure profit for imperialist nations and corporations through resource extraction and continued occupation. In short, colonial capitalism persists by deploying the mechanism of policing to repress resistance.

Next, we discuss how acts of defiance against colonial violence are used as a pretext for the further expansion of those very systems of domination. Here, the urgency of the call to defund is underscored by the continued expansion of police in both size and sophistication of weaponry while other sectors, such as education, are forced to practice austerity in the face of economic collapse. Moreover, Professor LeBrón discusses how the Puerto Rican government's platform Mano Dura Contra el Crimen ("Iron Fist Against Crime") exacerbates punitive policies as a form of social control of low-income neighborhoods comprised mostly of Afro-Latinx and Black residents. Ultimately, the enduring popularity of this practice serves to remind us that state violence is not only accepted but applauded by those who benefit from colonial capitalism because of how low-income communities of color have come to be seen as inherently dangerous and criminal.

Finally, we discuss social movements' international efforts at coalition-building, particularly in the aftermath of George Floyd's murder, as a form of decolonial, abolitionist praxis. We talk about the ways interpersonal violence can create conflict between oppressed groups, constituting an obstacle to this shared goal—one that we must strive to overcome by adopting a wider historical view of the colonial structures that underpin and uphold structural violence. In the end, we both agree that abolition praxis can shift discourse, see beyond the surface, and unite groups against the common enemy of colonial capitalism that is maintained through policing.

* * *

CJS: *Historically, policing on the island of Puerto Rico, continental United States, and other places around the globe show similar trends of violence, corruption, and targeting of racialized populations. How do you see the relationship between capitalism and policing manifest within "criminal justice" systems and law enforcement agencies?*

ML: First, policing facilitates colonialism *and* capitalism. While local instantiations might vary, we continue to see similar patterns emerge. Like Puerto Rico and the US, the same kind of policing occurs in places such as Brazil, South Africa, India, and the United Kingdom. Therefore, I think about the larger structural forces that undergird policing, rather than as isolated or individual entities.

Interestingly, there is something about policing that feels deliberately American. Yet, I think part of the issue is the way policing is framed, particularly by US scholars, as "made in the USA"—a mantra that is used as an explanation of why policing is fucked up everywhere. However, I would suggest this argument occludes the way that local elites [outside the US] benefit from policing that targets dissidents, reproduces racial disharmony, and keeps people economically subjugated. My work resists the urge to see Mano Dura Contra el Crimen as simply an importation of US policies in Puerto Rico.[45] In other words, the reason we see these overarching themes around policing is because policing itself is inherently problematic, not simply because of the US implementation.

Ultimately, my work challenges the fundamental purpose and need for police. In sum, I argue that policing is about maintaining colonial capitalism in Puerto Rico, and elsewhere, which creates stratification, particularly around race, class, and gender. Often, there are weak reformist arguments that claim policing can be improved, but this implicitly justifies the violent structure of police. For example, there are reductive arguments about the individual or isolated "bad" cop that went rogue, but this diminishes the reality of pervasive police violence. At the same time, these false narratives attempt to position police as "do-gooders," which is simply untrue as their primary function is to protect capital.

Finally, structural analysis is paramount for activists and scholars to think about how policing instantiates itself within local markets. For instance, what are the various iterations of how capitalism informs local policing? Further, how do various forms of crises within capitalism shift policing responses, often through violence? These questions are important to think through because it can be helpful to build alliances that combat police violence, such as the defund movement, and advocate the eradication of policing.

CJS: *In October 2021, on a panel hosted by the Schomburg Center for Research in Black Culture in Harlem, New York, you stated, "Policing as it impacts Puerto Rico is a model of the colonial crisis management," and, "Policing can function without the police." Could you provide some context for these statements, particularly as we look toward eradication. What are ways we could see policing without police?*

ML: The first part is related to the idea that policing in Puerto Rico is not about justice but rather managing crises that emerge because of colonial capitalism. There are numerous instances of police being used to attack labor strikes, student protests, and pro-independence movements. A common theme in all these examples is the challenge to colonial capitalism, which is met with arrests, tear gas, and beatings, highlighting that police create violence, not reduce it.

Further, there is an abundance of evidence of anti-Blackness within policing, in which Afro-Latinx and Black, low-income neighborhoods are targeted, particularly public housing, through surveillance and over-policing. I argue this is a form of politicized policing because it reifies larger frameworks of racialized punishment that view these populations as expendable in the ongoing "wars" on crime and drugs that manifest in the late twentieth century. Therefore, entire communities are disproportionately monitored and imprisoned as colonial capitalism responds to specific moments of crisis, whether financial austerity or a global pandemic.

The second part refers the legacy of Mano Dura Contra el Crimen. From 1993 to 2000, policing was meant to be showcased as spectacular, to demonstrate the capacity and power the government could wield. Consequently, policing became a sensationalized concept to "fight crime." Over time, the spectacular becomes the standard, and militarized zones with checkpoints, helicopter surveillance, and elite policing units that conduct routine raids are normalized as part of the life experience for residents in these low-income communities.

Now, twenty years later, crime is no better. In fact, in recent years, certain crimes in Puerto Rico have gotten worse. Therefore, the cultural logic and practices of Mano Dura Contra el Crimen must be interrogated. In other words, these spectacles created this idea that all Puerto Ricans are potential victims of crime. Yet, the data highlights that is not the case; rather, the people who are most at risk of experiencing violence are from the most marginalized sectors of Puerto Rican society: Black, low-income, gender-nonconforming folks, sex workers, and women. However, being inundated with crime rhetoric becomes a metonym for all of Puerto Rico, allowing this "us versus them" mindset that vilifies low-income folks of color, reinforcing racialized tropes of inherent criminality.

CJS: *Having been to Puerto Rico many times, I see these built environments with curated golf courses and gated communities establishing who is allowed into these spaces, creating barriers of physical proximity between Indigenous island residents and vacationers. Is this part of the legacy of Mano Dura Contra el Crimen?*

ML: I think it plays into it. But the social engineering that happened in the mid-twentieth century was supposedly about social uplift through proximity by placing low-income and working-class communities within the vicinity of middle- and upper-class areas as a sort of social osmosis of uplift. Zaire Z. Dinzey-Flores's book *Locked In, Locked Out: Gated Communities in a Puerto Rican City* discusses how gated communities emerged and proliferated throughout the 1980s.[46] Yet, by the 1990s, this social experiment is mostly abandoned, and gates with guardhouses and mechanical arms for cars are erected about these low-income neighborhoods, creating a demarcation of who the police should monitor that reinforces racial and class hierarchies.

Today, there is this additional layer of exclusion with the creation of these settler-colonial enclaves for "crypto bros," tax evaders, and others to have an artificial utopia for non-Indigenous tourists that are removed from the realities of everyday life in Puerto Rico.

CJS: *The failures of policing, whether in Puerto Rico or elsewhere, have led us to defund in the aftermath of George Floyd's murdered. Do you see defund as part of a larger decolonial project?*

ML: For sure. I remember being on a call with activists right after George Floyd was killed, and the discussion focused on defund—in particular, how defund fit into existing political landscapes. Puerto Rico's debt crisis is a prime example of how activists have been able to use defund to connect the contradictions in government austerity: the University of Puerto Rico system's budget is constantly being cut, but police continue to receive increased resources and funding.[47]

Further, defund recalls the 2019 protests demanding the removal of Governor Ricardo Rosselló,[48] as demonstrators recognized that there was money for police to tear-gas protesters amidst residents demanding accountability by leadership. Defund speaks to the longer colonial relationship between Puerto Rico and the US, as the island is consistently told there are no resources, aid, or relief, and the debt is framed as a personal responsibility. Yet, police are continually well equipped to exact violence. Ultimately, defund helps frame the paradox: Are there no funds and resources for the island and its people, *or* is it that these funds and resources are only given out to subdue and keep folks subjugated to colonial capitalist logics?

Programs such as Acuerdo de Paz in Loíza, which address violence through noncarceral mechanisms, constantly has its

budget cut.[49] Funds are funneled to police who, by design, protect capital. Therefore, any sort of resistance or "threat" to empire is punished. For example, Elimar Chardón Sierra, a former
music teacher, is under federal investigation because, after several budget cuts to educational programs and services, she called
a US federal judge and left a message saying something like, "I
hope you fucking die."[50] Subsequently, the FBI showed up and
charged her with making threatening calls over interstate tel-
ecommunication lines, highlighting the broad reach of colonial
capitalism. Sierra didn't say she was going to kill the judge but
simply expressed an emotion because of how this ruling directly
impacts her and her students' livelihood.

This case highlights how Puerto Ricans are pleading for
life-affirming services but are being dismissed. Yet, these decisions are not benign but have devastating impacts that are going
to kill people. Ultimately, police play a central role in making
sure that these laws and policies are upheld. Instead, defund
would provide an opportunity to shift budgets into other sectors
to provide resources, aid, and relief for residents.

CJS: *In summer 2020, protesters were connecting police violence to
larger forms of historical, structural, and symbolic violence. In Puerto Rico, demonstrators pointed out that many statues, plazas, and
cities were named after Spanish conquistadores.[51] While these sorts
of demands to remove these symbols are not new, does the motivation
change or become reinforced in the defund era?*

ML: That's interesting. I had not thought of this form of protest
in terms of defund, but I think it's related to this moment. There
is momentum around defund and the kind of protest for racial
justice, especially for many Black Puerto Ricans. For instance,
groups like Colectivo Ilé are doing work surrounding Blackness
in Puerto Rico.[52]

After George Floyd was killed, there were vigils and *bomba-
zos* [traditional dance gathering] in his memory in Puerto Rico,

opening space to talk about policing and Blackness in Puerto Rico. While movements on the island have always protested state violence, Mr. Floyd's death generated a link between activists in Puerto Rico and the US because anti-Black violence is pervasive in both places. Further, local activists have been smart about how they framed this connection. In other words, Blackness is not something that resides outside of Puerto Rico, and racism is present on the island.

In the weeks after George Floyd's death, various Puerto Rican musical artists produced songs highlighting these connections. Rafa Pabon's "Sin Aire" [Without Air] discusses the various deaths of Black men by police in the US but also discusses being Black in Puerto Rico and having to fear the police. In his music video, Pabon raps most of the song while being held down with a police officer kneeling on his neck—a direct reminder of what happened to George Floyd. He raps, "Solidaridad de parte del negro de Cupey," which translates to "solidarity from the Black folks of Cupey" [a barrio in Puerto Rico]. Additionally, Myke Towers released "Michael X," drawing parallels to Malcolm X and using images of slavery, the civil rights movement, and current police protests in his music video. He raps, "Abusaron cuando eramo' esclavos, eso nunca se nos olvida.... Orgulloso de ser negro, la gente sabe cómo soy," which translates to, "They abused us when we were slaves, we never forget that.... Proud to be Black, people know what I'm like." Here, he is offering this connection, which is sometimes forgotten, that slavery happened in Puerto Rico and that the slave legacies that impact Black Americans impact Afro–Puerto Ricans.

Lastly, while reggaeton has become very whitewashed in recent years, this moment became important to reinject the Black diaspora and radical discourse at the roots of the genre. It is building on discourses that folks like [Puerto Rican musician] Tego Calderón discussed.[53] The music not only shows solidarity but also highlights that Black folks in Puerto Rico are dealing with anti-Black police violence.

CJS: *In recent years, La Perla, a section of Old San Juan, has become a space of curious exploration by non–Puerto Rican residents. The area is associated with crime and violence but has been a site of American film and music. Yet, in early 2021, a Black American man was killed in La Perla.*[54] *Debate surrounding this murder unfolded on Twitter, highlighting division across spatial, ethnic, and racialized boundaries.*

Some Black Americans began to condemn the neighborhood, the island, and residents parroting much of the Mano Dura Contra el Crimen need for police. Conversely, some Puerto Rican residents began to entertain stereotypes of Black Americans being inherently criminal—in other words, that the only reason to be in La Perla would be to engage in nefarious acts—dismissing this death. Earlier, we talked about defund in a global context. How do we continue to keep people engaged and move forward when tragedies occur?

ML: The Twitter debate was horrible and frustrating, especially because it intersected with my research in tourism, policing, and race. It also created this false narrative of Black Americans versus Puerto Ricans, assuming all residents of the island are White, leaving Black Puerto Ricans out.

Many Afro–Puerto Ricans were infuriated by this discourse because it was an erasure of their existence, even though they are subjected to the same anti-Blackness, racism, and violence. There was also this interesting moment in the feud where Black Americans and [White] Puerto Ricans were both asking for more police under this fallacy of safety, which eliminates protection for Black Puerto Ricans. The reality is that Black American tourists were already safer than Indigenous Black populations on the island, as the concept of nationality was infused into the debate. While both the victim and perpetrator(s) are both technically

"American," there is something different that we can understand in the ability to claim "American" versus "Puerto Rican" identity.

Moreover, many Black Americans were right that much of the focus was on this idea of buying drugs. This narrative is an important component of "how policing can police without police" as it highlights the legacy of Mano Dura Contra el Crimen. The takeaway is that if you are a drug user, you deserve to die, and if you die, it's your fault. Weirdly, colonial capitalism makes violence acceptable if it happens to a drug user or someone engaging in illicit drug behavior.

Yet, folks need to remember that La Perla is not a tourist destination but a neighborhood of residents that has unwritten rules, which are coveted across global communities. However, because of tourist propaganda, the island is perceived as a place where you can do whatever the fuck you want, disregarding community rules. This is not to justify this man's demise but to highlight that even before this tragedy, La Perla residents were irritated with the dismalness of their way of life.

Overall, I think this debate intersects with the kind of conversations around defund, but also abolition. The call should not have been for more policing or military to take over a community, but to think deeply about what caused the violence to occur in that neighborhood in the first place—more specifically, how the state responds to, or neglects, violence, broadly.

This tragedy highlights the various kinds of iterations of colonial capitalism, where people who are in similar structural situations get pitted against each other in a variety of ways. Therefore, when conflicts arise, policing enters as some kind of de facto solution that is nonproductive and, in fact, exacerbates structural tensions, making solidarity difficult. In sum, police should not be our default to obtain justice.

Further, this topic reminds me that the music video "Despacito" by Luis Fonsi was partially shot in La Perla, highlighting how colonial capitalism attempts to sanitize these spaces to attract tourism for consumption. Then, when tragedies like this occur, it underscores the intersection of race, policing, colonialism, and nationalism, showcasing some of the worst in people.

The bigger takeaway is the loss of life and the myriad of circumstances that created the conditions that led to this tragedy. In sum, poverty, drug use, criminalization, and other factors did not happen the moment this individual stepped into La Perla but rather through centuries of anti-Blackness and decades of police violence. Therefore, I hope for both Black Americans and Black Puerto Ricans that this can be a source of recognition and solidarity amidst tragedy instead of division to challenge colonial hierarchies.

Finally, the optimism I hope for is the potential for abolitionist praxis in this moment to rightly point out that of Mano Dura Contra el Crimen police practices were already in this community but still didn't keep this person safe. This tragedy calls into question the role and presence of police to protect life, as this is another instance of that failure. Ultimately, abolition gives space to help move away from discourse, on both sides, surrounding inferiority and disposability, looking instead toward solidarity outside of conventional forms of police and punishment.

CJS: *Often, folks continue to forget that police are mostly reactive agents, not proactive. In other words, they are deployed after an incident occurs. We fail to imagine a society that creates spaces to be proactive and intervene through other means, prior to incidents taking place. This is something abolition is constantly working toward. To that end, how do you see the relationship between defund and the praxis of abolition? In other words, how do both terms land in this moment and, specifically, within the Latinx context?*

ML: I don't think the terms are the same, but they are related. Within an abolitionist practice and praxis, defund is complimentary, but abolition is not limited to that. In some recent conversations, I've seen this narrow liberal version of defund arise that only wants to move some money away from police. However, this is a short-sighted approach if that is the only goal. If defund is done right, it will eventually get to the point that we create something new.

[Critical criminologists] Megan McDowell and Luis Fernandez have this useful piece thinking about abolition in terms of policing, and they describe three actions: disband, disempower, and disarm.[55] Abolition is often thought about in terms of only prisons, but it is important to think about the abolition of the entire carceral state. The praxis must be uncompromising to reach the final goal, which is not simply to disarm police but to create a world where state-sanctioned violence is not possible. It is about holding on to that kind of utopian impulse of having something that seems far fetched until it becomes a reality.

CJS: *I suspect those who just want to decrease police budgets without addressing larger structural violence, and how law enforcement does this, would not be abolitionists but rather simply reformists. Maybe some identify as "radical" reformers?*

ML: It cannot just be cutting police budgets, but a larger reallocation of life-affirming resources. I'm optimistic that both groups [abolitionists and reformers] could work together, but I think standard reformist notions have been cynically deployed to squash certain kinds of abolitionist concepts. For example, the #8Can'tWait kind of reforms are not new reforms, because much of that rhetoric and action is already implemented in many police departments.[56] We also see how legislators have attempted to circumvent defund by moving money but into more police training and other liberal reforms.

CJS: *All things that have been shown not to work.*

ML: Exactly. Giving more money to police is not good, because police are the problem.

Defund is about shrinking police budgets down to nothing, which is an abolitionist praxis strategy. That is why these two terms are complementary, but I do think that there's a perversion of the term "defund," which is trying to "defang" and take the teeth out of the movement, which the movement must be prepared to combat.

It is interesting to see where Latinx folks fit into this debate, which has been interesting and frustrating because the experiences of Afro-Latinx and Black Latinos are often ignored. I'm currently working on a project that examines the history of how Latinos have experienced policing in the United States. One of the difficulties is framing the narrative; because "Latinos" is a fictitious category in many respects. Much like any racial or ethnic category, it is socially constructed. The term "Latino" brings together so many different people of various origins that it is difficult to capture an isolated "Latino" experience surrounding policing. Therefore, the argument I'm trying to make is that *policing* is what makes Latino a coherent category, because it is suffused in how we understand *latinidad* [Latino-ness] in the United States.[57] Whether it's policing the "illegal immigrants," "gang members," or "drug runners," it shapes and affects a certain type of "Latino" population.

I keep thinking about discussions in 2014 around Ferguson, Missouri, and Black Lives Matter and seeing signs reading "Latinos for Black Lives," which is an erasure of Afro-Latinos who experience policing in the US and their native countries. In some cases, it is the policing and state violence that makes them leave their homeland. These are the conversations I'm having with folks: to think about the Latinx experience regarding policing and where it intersects with longer-standing attempts to address police brutality and violence in the same way it impacts African Americans.

A few years ago, the *Los Angeles Times* produced a slew of articles that were attempting to argue that no one cares about

Latinos who are victims of police violence, because they're not Black. It was this insidious accusation but reaffirmed this idea that Latinos are not Black, creating this false mutual exclusivity. Yes, not all Latinos are Black, but there are Black Latinos, and their experience of policing is distinct from the experience of other (non-Black) Latinos. Moreover, this kind of anti-Black thinking ignores the ways in which we know that policing and race functions. Of course, Black folks experienced some of the worst forms of police violence, but it also spares no one, especially those who attempt to challenge capitalism or racial injustice.

For example, Kyle Rittenhouse, who was not a cop but masquerading as a law enforcement agent, killed two White activists [during August 2020 street protests in response to the police shooting of Jacob Blake, a Black man]. This case had overtones of racially motivated killings because the carceral logics for him to feel compelled to be in Kenosha, Wisconsin, are rooted in anti-Blackness. Therefore, from the perspective of the state, it does not matter that the activists killed are White, because they challenged the shooting of Jacob Blake, which was state-sanctioned violence.

These same carceral logics and state-sanctioned violence are seen on the southern US border—for example, arresting people leaving water for migrants, because this act of kindness is a threat to US colonial capitalism that challenges border logics.[58] I think about the depravity of arresting someone who is attempting to make sure others have basic human essentials such as water, so they don't die of dehydration. It is this mindset that makes defund possible and abolition an absolute.

CHAPTER 2

"Abolition as a 'Both/And' Project" with Dan Berger

D an Berger is a professor of comparative ethnic studies at the University of Washington, Bothell. His research focuses on critical race theory, social movements, and the histories of American incarceration policy and prison systems. Dan has written numerous books that explore the US carceral apparatus, with particular focus on Black Power, prison organizing, and political prisoners.[59] Our conversation examines the role the American prison system has played in shaping the current conditions that led to defund, as well as the future implications of defund for a larger abolitionist framework.

First, we unpack the ways in which various systems of captivity such as slavery, convict leasing, and mass incarceration converge and diverge. All of these systems share certain qualities of subjugation and oppression, but they are not the same: while slavery and convict leasing were developed to exploit labor, incarceration steals time.

Second, our conversation focuses on defining "political prisoner." In the current climate of heightened activism on both the left and the right, it is important to clearly articulate the relevance of this term for progressive, radical, and left politics. While it has historically been deployed by the left to identify comrades caught in the criminal legal system—sometimes for decades—many on the right also invoke the term, in spite of the very different circumstances of their prosecution by the state.

Next, we discuss the rich legacy of social movements that have sought to thwart carceral systems from within. Here, the architects of US prison movements, such as George Jackson[60] as well as the Free Alabama Movement,[61] provide examples that illustrate a spectrum of strategies and struggles toward liberation.

Finally, we turn our attention to the relevance of the term "defund" as a slogan, particularly in relation to abolitionism. Here, Dan echoes activist and educator Mariame Kaba in articulating that "#defund is the floor" that supports a long-term abolitionist movement. At same time, defund serves as a bridge between reformers and abolitionists. It is a multifaceted approach that looks beyond simply closing prisons and eradicating cops to envision a new society that emphasizes care, nonpunitive conflict resolution, and transformative justice.

* * *

CJS: *What are the connections between the institutions of slavery, convict lease system, and modern carceral state? Are all these systems tethered to the need of cheap labor? Can you elaborate on where you see them overlap as well as diverge from one another?*

DB: This is a huge question. And the reason for that, and why we should spend time unpacking it, is because there are some important and necessary connections for people to understand between slavery and incarceration—not just *mass* incarceration, but simply incarceration itself.

There are some misapplications of those connections, and one way that people misunderstand that connection between slavery and incarceration is to see it as an unbroken continuation of coerced labor. [Geographer] Ruth Wilson Gilmore's work eloquently highlights that the point of prisons, particularly in the second half of the twentieth century, is to steal not labor but time.[62] Prisons are warehouses, primarily and disproportionately composed of people of color in the prime working years of their lives, precisely because they have been written out of the formal economy. In most prisons today, people are not working for profit or producing anything of value with their labor. Therefore, we are dealing with the exploitation of time. People's lives are being stolen by the state, and it creates this idleness filled with the ever-presence of violence, but also of boredom. Even for folks who do have prison jobs, it is typically not an eight-hour workday but rather a few hours a couple times per week, in some places—such as here, in Washington [State].

Often, if folks are working, it is to socially reproduce the prison, such as working in the kitchen or cleaning the yard—something [anthropologist] David Graeber calls "bullshit jobs."[63] This distinction between slavery and incarceration is important for a lot of reasons. During slavery, but also convict leasing, people were being held in captivity or arrested and sent to plantations or prisons, respectively, to extract their labor. That is not happening now. People aren't being arrested for mass production of license plates, whereas in the 1870s, for example, the Tennessee Coal, Iron, and Railroad Company needed workers, and convict leasing coerced individual labor under the guise of criminal justice.[64]

All this to say: labor is not the connection that some have argued. The through line of incarceration that connects to slavery is *captivity*. People's lives and sense of self-determination is contained and confined by forces outside of their control. Slavery was about the master–slave relationship that was approved by the state. Imprisonment is this kind of machine that moves people from arrest to incarceration, that reshapes their relationship with the state. It is this sense of captivity that connects the deeply entrenched infrastructure of slavery with its afterlives in the form of mass incarceration that is informed by racism, which has been the entirety of US existence.

Ultimately, what animates mass incarceration, and the warehouse model of incapacitation, is the repression of Black rebellion and other progressive movements, combined with the restructuring of the economy that dismisses the already most marginalized people from the formal employment sector.

CJS: *It becomes about disposability. During slavery, an enslaved person held an intrinsic value as a commodity that could be put up as collateral—insurance—sold, or traded. The end goal within that system was not to kill a person but to exploit them. Conversely, bodies held in prison facilities do not have that same inherent value, so if life is lost in a place such as Rikers Island,[65] there is no fundamental disruption of the economy. If that assessment is accurate, how does this shift the dynamics surrounding social movements and prison organizing today?*

DB: Exactly, there are challenges to how incarcerated people organize. The national prison strike in 2016, which started with the Free Alabama Movement at Holman Prison, is an example of that direct connection to slavery as many Southern prisons use coerced labor from imprisoned individuals. A centerpiece of this movement was a call to "let the crops rot in the fields," and this gave those inside leverage to highlight that without them, the prison system does not run efficiently.[66] It was a classic labor strategy. Unfortunately, this tactic is not generalizable to all prisons across the country, nor does it necessarily contain the same disruptive power as a strike outside of prisons.

In other words, even if every person in prison refused to work, it would not bring down prisons, because the system is primarily operating out of an orientation toward repression, not labor. So we must be careful about how we approach strikes and organizing because of possible regional differences. Folks in California and Michigan have had their own versions of a strike, and the primary focus was not labor but rather health care, food, solitary confinement, and abuse by guards.[67] Obviously, those incarcerated are the most directly impacted by whatever strategy is applied, and we need to be ready to follow their lead and support their actions. However, this reinforces the concept of prisons as mainly warehousing bodies through repression, not for profit; and when you are not profitable, you are disposable. Hence, we see the tragedies of lost life in places like Rikers and other facilities across the country.

CJS: *I often associate prison movements with political prisoners. Could you discuss what it means to be a political prisoner and how someone is given this title?*

DB: This is a complicated question. Some might argue that everyone in prison is a political prisoner. I don't find that position to be helpful. I do agree that everyone in prison is incarcerated for political reasons since prosecutors and judges are often elected officials running on certain campaign platforms. Further, sentencing schemas are decided by legislative bodies, so there are lots of political dynamics that go into the context of someone's incarceration. But that doesn't mean someone automatically becomes a political prisoner.

Political prisoners are criminalized and incarcerated for their involvement in social movements and recognizing that the law is used in a targeted and disproportionate way to punish those who violate political or economic norms. Often, we see individuals given outrageously long sentences when involved in a movement deemed "leftist."

Conversely, I have been following how so many of the January 6 insurrectionists who attacked the US Capitol [in 2021] are receiving relatively light punishments compared to folks on the left, who have been found guilty of far less. Most of the January 6 defendants have gotten a few months in prison. So far, I think the most serious sentence I saw was five years for someone who engaged in physical violence such as attacking cops and destruction of government property.[68]

This is the same amount of time that Crystal Mason, a Black woman in Texas, received for voting when she wasn't allowed because she was on parole.[69] While Crystal does not fit the mold of traditional activist, she is still a political prisoner. Similarly, Jessica Reznicek, an environmental activist, was sentenced to eight years, which included a terrorism enhancement charge, for destruction of an oil pipeline.[70] Finally, two lawyers in New York City, Colin Mattis and Urooj Rahman, were facing literally decades in prison for the destruction of police property during the summer 2020 protests.[71]

I've written about 1960s, '70s, and '80s social movements and people who have received lengthy, if not life, sentences. Yet, at the same time, many White Power militants, the forerunners to January 6, such as abortion bombers and homophobic killers, were either acquitted or received little to no jail time in comparison.

CJS: *The term "political prisoner" evokes a certain leftist ideology. Yet, could that term be applied to these sorts of right-wing individuals who have been arrested or imprisoned, or do they fall outside the "political prisoner" typology?*

DB: Several right-wing politicians and pundits attempted to make this claim, such as huckster opportunists in Congress like Marjorie Taylor Greene. She became critical of the [Washington] DC jail system when her constituents were locked in these horrible conditions but didn't give a shit about the mostly Black DC residents who are held in confinement for far less serious offenses than trying to overthrow an election.

I'm, appropriately, unsettled by this position. Yet, one cannot deny that January 6 insurrectionists were engaged in a political movement—obviously one that I find abhorrent and unconscionable—but yes, their arrest happened in the context of participation in a political movement, which is why I think it's important to carve out and define "political prisoner."

Looking at the international definition of "political prisoner," it was developed in the context of liberation struggles, such as participation against racism and colonialism. In the US, folks like Mumia [Abu-Jamal] and Leonard Peltier, amongst others, would fit this international definition that Klansmen, neo-Nazis, and QAnon would not. So it is worth recognizing that these right-wing groups are part of a political movement and encountering the legal system, but only to the extent to which they face punishment—which is vastly different than people on the left struggling *against* systems of oppression, rather than fighting to *reinforce* systems of repression, as they do on the right.

Finally, we cannot define "political prisoners" too narrowly, as there are people who did not go to prison for a political reason but joined a social movement on the inside and contributed to shaping prison movements. Probably the most famous example is George Jackson.

CJS: *This reminds me of the 2013 California state prison hunger strike, which was started by gang leaders from various racial backgrounds.*

DB: That was a huge moment in prison organizing; because the California prison system takes advantage of using race to govern and maintain repression in their facilities. This was powerful because the leaders of these different groups came together to say that the actual problem is the system itself, not racial division.

Going back, George Jackson, widely seen as a Black Nationalist, talks about the fundamental need for incarcerated people to come together as a class to overthrow the state, starting with the prison system. He advocated a multiracial, revolutionary armed struggle and recognized how racism is used as a barrier to stifle this alliance. And it is not a coincidence this strike happened in the California prison system, the same in which he was imprisoned, highlighting that his teachings still hold relevance amongst his would-be peers.

CJS: *The same can be said about the Black Panthers, who are often reduced to "Black guys with guns" but were much more in line with Marxist ideology. For instance, Fred Hampton's Rainbow Coalition brought together various political and street-level organizations across racial lines.*

In recent years, political prisoners such as Jalil Muntaqim, Herman Bell, and David Gilbert, as well as the living members of the MOVE 9, have been released. Yet Mumia Abu-Jamal, Sundiata Acoli,[72] and Leonard Peltier are still incarcerated. Do you have optimism that things are changing—that the "old guard" that has kept these individuals locked up for nearly a half century are being replaced and that they might be released?

DB: I use this term "carceral federalism," which understands the relationship of power of the federal government relative to the states. In sum, states are doing one thing, and the federal government is doing nothing, or something else. Look at the death penalty, which most states have moved away from but which the federal government retains. We must recognize federalism in the prison context; because most people are incarcerated in state, not federal, prisons. This means, for example, we cannot petition the president to free Mumia. Only the governor of Pennsylvania could grant Mumia clemency because of where he was convicted and sentenced.

Moreover, you mentioned several people who were all imprisoned in New York, and there were some amazing organizers who worked hard to transform, or at the very least shift, the New York parole board as well as pressure the governor to release individuals through pardons and commute sentences.[73]

Folks began to point out the politicized nature of the parole board and how the FOP [Fraternal Order of Police] and other pro-cop organizations dominated the parole boards. More specifically, people were not being released due to the "nature of their crime," and of course that is a betrayal to the principle of parole; because the crime never changes. The board is charged to review behavior and time incarcerated and decide release based on how one spent their time inside. It was efforts toward changing this culture of parole that got folks like Jalil, Herman, and Robert Seth Hayes released.[74] David Gilbert's case was slightly different because he was given clemency, which then made him eligible for parole; because he was originally sentenced without the possibility of parole. Also, I think the MOVE example, out of Pennsylvania, also required organizing at the state level and using an impressive political and legal strategy that resulted in their freedom.

For folks like Mumia and Leonard—two of the most famous political prisoners of that generation—it is a bit trickier. Mumia's case must be contextualized in the framework of Philadelphia and the city's political machine, which is unfortunately an uphill battle. This is similarly the case for Leonard Peltier because, like Mumia, he is incarcerated for allegedly killing police. Peltier is in federal prison, and Bill Clinton has been the closest in considering releasing him—in 2000, at the end of his term—but the FBI staged a huge protest and Clinton moved away from it.[75]

My last point on this is to reiterate how people have fought hard to organize and transform the political conditions that have resulted in meaningful change. This includes those we mentioned, who advocated for their own release and continue to organize on behalf of others. I've been inspired by the #BringSundiataHome campaign, which has picked up a lot of momentum in the last year. Since this case happens to be in New Jersey, I'm hopeful this campaign will be victorious. [Sundiata Acoli was released in May 2022.]

CJS: *Do you think the carceral state needs these individuals as a sort of poster image to continue to expand repression and state-sponsored surveillance?*

DB: Sure. It relies on these sorts of spectacles of punishment and abuse—that if you get out of line, your autonomy will be taken by the state—as well as the threat of violence experienced in the facility. For example, we hear jokes like "Don't drop the soap," which is alluding to the sexual violence baked into these systems.

It's the same reason that when abolition is brought up, people automatically bring up serial killers. In Washington [State], Gary Ridgway, known as the Green River Killer, is the poster child of why we can't get rid of prison and "What are we going to do with people like him?" Therefore, serial killers are important to the "true crime" genre as a sort of staple for prisons because it feeds this imaginary of ever-present danger. The same is true for sex offenders: there is no proactive attempt to deal with the danger, only a reactive attempt to conjure a new specter of danger requiring carceral authority and control.

CJS: *Going back to social movements: your article in the* Boston Review *about the internationalism of SNCC [Student Nonviolent Coordinating Committee][76] made me think about Malcolm X meeting Fidel Castro in Harlem in 1960, as well as more recent international solidarity movements in which activists across the globe communicate and share strategies via social media in real time.[77] Why is it important to incorporate an international perspective in organizing, and how do we continue to forge these relationships, even when there might be divergent end goals?*

DB: What I find so interesting is how international movements of the '60s to '80s were without contemporary technology but made it work. I remember doing an interview with someone who had been imprisoned as a draft resister, and the first time they learned about the Holocaust and the Dachau concentration camp was by reading George Jackson's writings. Further, Jackson wrote about apartheid in South Africa. This is incredibly important because it is the parallels between the United States and the Union of South Africa, that Jackson uses to make connections to White supremacy as a global system that must be challenged and dismantled. Further, there are murals of Angela Davis and various Black Panther members in Ireland, Palestine, and South Africa, highlighting an international anti-colonialism.

About a decade ago, a "Free Mumia" group in Germany invited me to give a talk, and afterward someone who had belonged to the Red Army Faction asked if I knew Susan Rosenberg—a political prisoner released by Clinton—and said, "When I was in prison, we would write to each other, but we lost contact after our release. Please give her my love." Similarly, the late political prisoner and activist Marylin Buck was well known for her international correspondences while imprisoned. Folks saw themselves in this broader context of international struggle that subverted national borders. Today, work around Palestinian political prisoners has been significant and become a key part of a global left organizing that is inspiring—especially the aspects of resisting the carceral state.

CJS: *There is an illusion that the United States is, by default, the perfect model and everything else is wrong. However, whenever problems with the US model are raised folks have excuses or think it will just organically get better—especially in the context of policing and prisons. Conversely, when more leftist struggles and progressive approaches "fail," there is this "Well, you should give up on that" mentality. For example: policing doesn't work, but any mention of ending this institution is met with ferocious, reactionary responses. In sum, it seems like the rope for police is infinite. Meanwhile, alternative systems are given a limited trial and immediately shut down at the first sign of an issue.*

DB: Yep, that is the kind of anticipatory logic of the carceral state—this idea that there is always lurking danger, which primes people for fear. More importantly, carceral logic is used to justify violent responses by law enforcement, regardless of level of threat to police or broader society in any given situation. In other words, the state can sanction violence indiscriminately in the name of "safety."

It reminds me of an interview I did with [civil rights and anti-war activist] Laura Whitehorn for an article in *TruthOut*.[78] She explained that most people in prison are there for who they were when they did it and less for what they did. If you are deemed a leftist radical, that threatens the conventional norms; your punishment will reflect that. Our current system thrives on subjugation, whereas abolition is experimental. It is an urgent sense that the current order is bad and gives us hope to move forward with an alternative, which is not premised on any specific dichotomous framing that must be a US or other existing model. Abolition centers the problems and allows us to focus on the world we need, not simply recreating the world we have.

CJS: *I'm glad you brought up abolition; because, as a concept, it goes beyond what we can see, to what we can imagine. I think the most exciting part about an abolitionist paradigm is that it frees us from a sort of limited vision.*

Given the rise of defund and how it became paired with calls for abolition of the police, prisons, and other oppressive systems, do you see defund as a mo(ve)ment? Are defund and abolition synonymous, complimentary, dichotomous, or something else?

DB: I envision defund as both a movement and moment. As Mariame Kaba has adamantly and correctly professed, especially on Twitter, #defund is the floor, not the ceiling. Therefore, I think framing defund as a movement *and* moment is important. For a long time, groups like Critical Resistance, and people such as Angela Davis and Ruth Wilson Gilmore, seemed like the lone voice in the wind opposing mass incarceration, because more prisons continued to be built and cops hired. However, shifts began after the 2008 financial crisis, which gave opportunities to rewrite the narrative of how people understood the function of policing, role of prisons, and how both are anchored to a broader political economy.

While living in Philadelphia, I was part of starting Decarcerate PA in 2011, a grassroots coalition that attempted to stop new prison construction. We had dozens of organizations endorse our platform within weeks. Even though we failed to stop prison construction, I'm convinced that our organizing contributed to Republican governor Tom Corbett losing his reelection bid in 2014 by wide margins, at a time when Tea Party was capturing statehouses around the country. It also helped create the context for [reformist Democrat] Larry Krasner to become Philadelphia's district attorney. While this is not abolition, these victories only occurred because of the kinetic energy of movements that strategize with abolition in mind.

Moreover, I cannot stress the importance of framing movements when creating a dialogue around concepts that most people are unfamiliar with. For instance, if I stood on a street corner and chanted "Abolish prisons," passersby might not know what I'm talking about. But if I shift my chant to "Don't build more prisons," folks understand those words and might engage in a discourse; now we are talking about decarceration and how we should let more people out. Because the problem of prison overcrowding is not solved by more prisons; rather, the problem of prison overcrowding is solved by letting folks out. This conversation can now advance abolitionist goals. Defund functions similarly because the idea of defunding the police has existed before 2020, but it achieved a level of visibility, popularity, and understanding that was not previously around, even in 2019.

CJS: *Like the divest movement that pressures institutions to get out of the business of investing in prisons or companies that use prison labor.*

DB: Exactly.

It's important to recognize how folks come to abolition. There are individuals who have been abolitionists for a long time and have pointedly argued reform does not work. However, most people come to abolition through trial and error as various reforms such as diversity trainings, body-worn cameras, and community-complaint review boards did not reduce state-sanctioned violence. In fact, police killings have risen. Therefore, the "trial and error" journey is what made the 2020 moment so powerful and why I'm a proponent of defund, not only politically, but as a slogan; because it's very powerful. I laugh at the think pieces that attempt to argue how wrong defund is, which, to me, makes it that much more relevant.

Unlike many reform efforts—which are designed, I believe, in some cases, with the best of intentions—defund cannot be co-opted as a slogan in the same way. It is literally, at the floor level, about taking away funding and resources from police and putting it into other sectors of society. Defund comes out of these deeper roots of people doing abolitionist work because it highlights how police have too much power, which is underwritten and granted this expansive authority through their budgets and resources.

To this end, defund pushes back at the ever-expanding criminal justice system and was a *moment*; because it was the largest protest in US history bringing together first-time protesters with seasoned activists. There is, now, this pre-2020 and post-2020 moment for many. Defund is also a *movement* because it has spawned new efforts and organizations, such as the initiative to defund the Minneapolis Police Department through the democratic process. Even though it didn't work, it came very close—which is optimistic, moving forward. Across the country, folks are running for local office on abolitionist tickets. And while protests have died down, there are widespread mutual aid networks that continue, and communities are taking a keener look at local budgets and even, if not changing it, at the very least questioning it—which plants the seeds ahead.

CJS: *The vote in Minneapolis not passing goes back to what I had mentioned earlier—that for liberals, it was seen as a failure. But I agree with you. It was revolutionary to even have that vote to begin with.*

DB: Right, we must contextualize this in relationship between the rise of defund and the direct backlash in the form of anti-CRT [critical race theory], which is an anti-intellectual project formed by right-wing fascism. Ultimately, the reactionary politics highlights how the right understands defund, in terms of power. Behind this bevy of anti-protest and anti-CRT bills is the inaction by the center right, liberals, and mainstream media because of how defund threatens the status quo.

CJS: *Beyond these reactionary bills, we have seen the role of the courts in the aftermath of summer 2020 protests—for example, the acquittal of Kyle Rittenhouse, as well as the conviction of the three White men who killed Ahmaud Arbery.[79] How should organizers and coalitions understand Rittenhouse's case in the longer legacy of violence toward activists? Moreover, is the conviction of the three men who killed Arbery a form of justice, even within the apparatus that we are advocating must be destroyed?*

DB: Honestly, I'm pessimistic about the justice question; because there is no justice for Ahmaud Arbery. He was hunted by racists while jogging, and the system tried covering it up. However, to the extent to which people consider the legal system as a barometer of sanctioning behavior, I suppose it is better they were convicted than acquitted.

To that end, these men have made no attempt to apologize or atone for the harm they caused, and any discussion of justice must begin with responsibility. Danielle Sered's book *Until We Reckon*, about restorative and transformative justice, discusses how prisons prevent accountability because the state intervenes to punish and people who have committed violent harm never have to take accountability.[80] Those convicted interact with police, courts, and corrections but never with the individuals, families, or communities in which the harm was committed. To my knowledge, this is what is occurring in the Arbery case. These men engaged in a modern lynching, have been convicted, and will be incarcerated, without ever having to ask for redemption.

In the context of abolition, it is not simply about removing prisons but also about removing the idea that our response to social problems is and *ought to be* prisons. We must contend with the fact that we live in a society that allowed for this murder to occur and a lot of injustice and blame to go around.

Turning to Rittenhouse: it connects back to our earlier discussion about the politics of who goes to prison. This teenager talked openly about his ambitions to be a police officer and, in that moment, took it upon himself to act as cop. His case highlights the idea of how much power police have, even without the formal badge, as his case was framed as a young man coming to the rescue to suppress a rebellion.

I ponder: If Rittenhouse was convicted, would Ahmaud's killers have been acquitted? It might sound conspiratorial, but we must remember the district attorney in Ahmaud's case was not moving forward with any plans to indict until the video surfaced, went viral, and enormous social pressure was placed on the DA's office. It's almost like this sort of balance, of "Each side gets one."

CJS: *Finally, how do we sustain abolition movements moving forward?*

DB: Much of my work examines the carceral state and why it is bad—particularly how it is a tool of political and social repression. More importantly, the carceral state cannot solve the problems it claims to resolve but only responds to the problems it has created.

This is important to abolition, and I'm inspired by restorative and transformative justice as well as mutual aid collectives because abolition is a "both/and" project, rather than an "either/or" mission. It is a rejection of these dichotomous or binary, zero-sum approaches. We are not going to solely "mutual aid" ourselves to abolition, but mutual aid is certainly a component of abolitionism. Therefore, to sustain abolition we need to fight on all fronts. This might mean mutual aid, fighting to free people from prison, stopping further prison construction, defunding the police, engaging in restorative and transformative justice practices, engaging in local politics, and collectives, such as growing our own food in community gardens. It also means fighting for things like universal health care and nuclear disarmament. All this becomes part of the "both/and" strategy toward abolition; because none of these things happen in isolation.

Another part of an abolitionist strategy is transforming ourselves: How do we grow our own capacity to prevent harm, respond to conflict and deal with conflict in nonpunitive ways, prevent state violence, and strategically organize?

[Labor activist and scholar] Jane McAlevey, among others, has discussed the need to organize education and health care workers.[81] In any society, the need for education and health care is fundamental, and creating jobs that are necessary, meaningful, and dignified makes sense. But this alone will still be inefficient if other things are not changed. Therefore, I appreciate defund because it opens the door to conversations about budgets and spending, with the priority of removing police and prisons, and understanding that many other areas of our society need attention, funding, and resources. Defund powerfully showed the inverse relation between policing and social spending. It showed what, and who, this country's elites value. We've got to tear down and build up at the same time—to devise new ways of relating to each other. For example, the Green New Deal, or any kind of climate remediation policy, is about creating livable futures for everybody. The COVID-19 pandemic has continued to underscore that public health only matters if it includes everybody. The moment segments of society are neglected, such as those incarcerated, a catastrophic imbalance occurs.

The pandemic has revealed the necessity of abolitionist projects because the virus does not discriminate. Therefore, strategies that protect everyone must be implemented. Recognizing this interconnection of movements across various fronts, whether confronting state-sanctioned violence in the form of police and prisons, climate change, or public health, all are connected to defund as a "both/and" strategy to sustain abolition.

CHAPTER 3

"Community Is a Verb" with Zellie Imani

Z ellie Imani is a teacher, journalist, community organiz-er, cofounder of Black Lives Matter–Paterson (New Jer-sey),[82] and cofounder of the Black Liberation Collective. During our discussion, we talk about the vital role activism plays in community organizing and how defund and abolition are nec-essary in these practices.

We begin by talking about how he came to activism, specifi-cally the impactful role of his parents, community, and occupa-tion as a public schoolteacher. Further, we address the funda-mental necessity of mutual aid as Zellie unpacks this concept and applies it to his notion that "community is a verb"—that the collective actions taken by individuals and groups to ensure pub-lic safety, harm reduction, and protect residents from police and state-sanctioned violence.

From here, our conversation turns to BLM-Paterson, specif-ically the "Black Lives Matter" mural painted on the streets of Paterson, the role music and creative expression play in inclusive organizing, and how 2020 became a pivotal moment in social movements as organizers had to address public health concerns with the onset of the COVID-19 pandemic. This leads us to talk about defund as an organizing strategy. Here, Zellie highlights how defund is a powerful moment within a broader movement, articulating the ways policing and mass incarceration are intrinsically connected.

We then discuss the strategic role of social media in organizing, before concluding with importance of addressing one's own mental health. After all, to stay committed to community work, one must make sure they are prioritizing their personal needs, too. Zellie sums this up best when he states we must learn that " 'no' is a complete sentence."

* * *

CJS: *Who inspired your work as a community activist?*

ZI: My parents inspired my activism because they were activists in college, engaging in sit-in movements in the 1970s to increase Black faculty, such as [poet] Nikki Giovanni, and [Black] students at Rutgers [University]. They showed me what it means to be a Black person in America, how Black people are treated, and the role I could play in changing the world. From an early age, I was learning about slave rebellions, civil rights leaders, and the Black Panthers. In school, we learned about Dr. King, but at home, I was learning about Nat Turner, Frederick Douglass, Huey P. Newton, and Malcolm X. This influenced my philosophy and practices going forward. Today, I would say my biggest inspiration is our ancestor Ella Baker.

CJS: *The legacy of Black student unions is important to understand why we have Africana studies and ethnic studies departments at institutions of higher learning today. It was because of the sacrifices of those who came before us, not some altruism by these institutions.*

ZI: Right.

It's funny because people talk about Samuel L. Jackson the actor, but less folks know about Samuel L. Jackson the student activist, who held members of the Morehouse College board of trustees hostage, demanding changes to curriculum. This led to him being kicked out of the school. Therefore, I wholeheartedly understand the sacrifices made so that you and I could have a better experience and more opportunities.

CJS: *For sure, he was really a bad you-know-what back in the day!*

Besides activism, you are also public schoolteacher. How does being a Black male in a space that overwhelmingly lacks representation of Black men connect your teaching and activism?

ZI: There is a direct link, because the school is not separate from the community. I teach in a community in which I was born and raised. Therefore, I have a vested interest in all the students, not just those in my classroom.

I am the only Black male instructor and teach fourth grade math at a public school in Paterson. The students interact with me differently because I approach them as human beings and show them respect and love, which is reciprocated. Every morning, all the kindergarteners give me a [fist] pound. Same goes for the eighth graders and everyone in between; because I have forged relationships, and they see me in solidarity with them.

I approach teaching from my own experiences and the ability to relate to Black teachers growing up. It is about being a positive force in their lives and doing the small things, like saying "good morning," because sometimes that makes all the difference. Unless a student tells us, we don't know what's going on for them outside of school.

Additionally, I facilitate a restorative justice program, which intervenes in conflicts. For example, we did a healing circle with eighth graders after an incident with racial undertones. The students believed they were being targeted by school administrators for speaking up, and our program gives them space to discuss their emotions in a controlled environment. More specifically, the students felt that teachers were not taking their concerns seriously and downplayed the incident. What we learned from the healing circle is that students want to be heard and not immediately blamed any time they speak up.

CJS: *I first learned of your work in fall 2014 when my students, particularly those in the Black Student Union, began mobilizing in response to the non-indictments in both the Michael Brown and Eric Garner cases. Since then, I have followed you on social media and the work you have done, including harm reduction programs, community refrigerators, the BLM summer youth camp, immediate responder campaigns, stop-blood-loss initiatives, and so much more.[83] Why is this work important, and how does it foster community cohesion and collective movement building?*

ZI: My comrades and I discuss how the Black Lives Matter movement is seen as only responding to police violence, but that's not all we are doing. Yes, we are fighting for people whose lives are lost, but also fighting for the people who are still alive.

Black Lives Matter's guiding principle is about recognizing all Black people's humanity, not just folks killed. We fight against systems that are destroying our neighborhoods as well as work to build alternative communities that provide resources to residents. Ultimately, when government and business can't figure it out, we step in to ensure that people are going to be fed during a global pandemic, reduce the amount of overdose deaths due to the opioid crisis, and seek a world without police.

Regarding the last point, that does not mean a world without safety, but a world without harm. We want to get rid of this system and show people that there are viable alternatives. We can protect our own communities and keep each other safe without having to rely on police. Our work is to accomplish much of these endeavors through mutual aid efforts.

CJS: *Could you elaborate on the term "mutual aid" and what it means? Also, you often sign a lot of your social media posts with the phrase "community is a verb." Could you talk about what this means in the context of being an organizer?*

ZI: Mutual aid is a philosophy and practice.[84] It stems from the idea that if I have a resource that you need, I'll share that resource with you. Under capitalism, there is an individualistic mindset that we are in competition because of this illusion that there is a scarcity of resources. This creates a world in which some get further ahead by hoarding resources or knowledge. Mutual aid dismantles that idea by saying we do not get ahead by being in competition with one another but rather by supporting each other through shared resources.

Moreover, when we say, "Community is a verb," it is about building relationships, especially in moments of crisis. Often, folks suffer in silence and isolation. In community, we can come together and help each other. We saw this isolated suffering in the early days of the pandemic. People who were immune compromised or had other health-related problems were being cut off—in some cases forgotten. If I'm going to the grocery store and can pick up items for a neighbor, that highlights "community is a verb." It is about the actions we can do for each other. The pandemic forced us to think and make shifts to the work we are doing.

As organizers, we know that protest momentum slows over time. Instead of hanging it up, we build connections and support each other through our "community is a verb" model. This way, when the unfortunate, but inevitable, next police killing occurs, that galvanizes marches and protests; we are stronger. Often, during moments of protest, folks go to a rally and then disperse without ever knowing the person next to them. If we are not building with those immediately next to us, then we are not recognizing the humanity around us. We need to be able to connect and utilize our collective skills. Ultimately, mutual aid gives us these tools to embrace "community is a verb."

CJS: *What has activism looked like during the pandemic, and what are some of the lessons you have learned that you will take with you moving forward?*

ZI: One lesson that I hope everyone learned is that the government has resources to support folks in our country. Early in the pandemic, BLM-Paterson made demands to cancel rent, and people were looking at us like we had three heads. But now, we see people coming around to this idea of rent moratoriums and pausing evictions. People need housing, and the country didn't implode when the landlords didn't get rent. In fact, billionaires grew their personal wealth.[85]

Unfortunately, because of government failure, at all levels, to act quickly, the community had to step up and fill that void. COVID-19 did not create the disparities we see in our communities but rather exacerbated them. BLM-Paterson created an infrastructure, through mutual aid, to help folks during the lockdown because people, especially elders, needed food and medicine. However, the pandemic opened a lot of eyes to possibilities that had previously been thought impossible. It's not that the government can't provide resources; they just choose not to.

CJS: *The discussion of mutual aid makes me think about the other end of the spectrum, such as charity, where some have hoarded all types of resources and are positioned to select who receives funding. We often see these types of people, organizations, and companies applauded. When a billionaire gives away a million dollars as charity, there is still a level of stratification because the money is being given to those who are seen as "below."*

ZI: Correct. That's the trouble with charity: it creates hierarchy that proclaims worth and dictates who receives money and resources. Unfortunately, what happens is, people and communities who are deserving don't obtain what is needed for survival. We need to have a framework that puts forth that everyone is deserving of support, love, care, and resources, as opposed to a selected few, as tokens, for charity.

Also, charity creates an internal mindset that folks might not believe they are deserving of resources because maybe they are not homeless, abusing substances, or engaged in survival sex work. It creates this notion that people who are poor tell themselves, "I'm poor, but I'm not *that* poor." Our organizing efforts have found that people become hesitant to accept help or take something they need, and we constantly remind folks, "You need this as well. It is okay." Everyone needs a meal to survive. We shouldn't base our food intake by who is hungriest but rather acknowledge that food is a vital resource for all. We emphasize that you don't have to feel like you can only accept mutual aid support when you are at the bottom, because everyone is deserving.

CJS: *In summer 2020, BLM-Paterson painted "Black Lives Matter" in bold yellow font as a mural on a city street. Why are actions like this important to movements, and what would be your response to criticisms that say efforts like these are performative?*

ZI: Oh man, that mural was a battle; because we wanted it right in front of the police department but got pushback from the mayor and city council. They told us we could put it anywhere else except in from of the police department, because it would cause division and make officers upset. Why would a statement that reads "Black Lives Matter," in a city where roughly a third of the population identifies as Black, upset the police? In the end, we made a compromise, and the mural was next door, on the site of an Underground Railroad stop. Symbolically, that concession was important as a site of the original Black Lives Matter movement[86] and continuing that legacy toward abolition.

Further, the mural was extremely important for community-building. It wasn't simply painting the street. The entire community came out, from small children to elders. People passing by saw what we were doing and took a paintbrush or a roller to do a couple strokes so they could be involved. This is what we are saying when we talk about "community is a verb." It doesn't matter if you were out there all three days or just a few minutes; folks put some of themselves down on the street. While some might say this act is simply performative, it meant something for a lot of people in the community to contribute.

CJS: *Adding to art and expression: the late Pop Smoke's single "Dior" became the official anthem of summer 2020. On July 26, 2020, you posted an amalgamation of protest videos where this song was being used by activists and in the comments wrote, "I love us all of us together. We will win. #M4BL #blacklivesmatter" Why do you think "Dior" was so important to this movement, and particularly that moment?*

ZI: Movements have always been led by the youth, and that song was the summer vibe. Organizing is about inclusivity, and not only those who understand theory or "best practices" but also street folks off the corner who have no idea who Karl Marx or Ella Baker are but understand the energy and want to win together. If someone wants to jump on the mic and cursing is part of their vernacular, we aren't going to police their language or enforce respectability politics. Our goal is to recognize each other's humanity. It doesn't matter how you talk, dress, or music you listen to, because there is no right thing to listen to or form of expression.

Across the country, we saw folks in the streets from all walks of life. During demonstrations, people heard music and began dancing, voguing, moving, and cheering each other on. That collective spirit was inspiring because folks were recognizing humanity. We all saw the police in their militarized riot gear, ready to use violence, and we were in that space ready to protect each other. Even rival gang sets were standing in unison and recognized the common enemy were police.

CJS: *Since 2020, the terms defund and "abolition" have grown in our popular lexicon. Do you see defund as a moment or movement, and are these terms synonymous, complimentary, dichotomous, or something else?*

ZI: Defund is a movement as well as a powerful moment. I'm excited that defund has become part of the broader conversation because many of us have been talking about abolition for a long time, but it has been on the fringe. However, folks have embraced defund as a strategy to get us on the path toward abolition.

Unfortunately, what happens, specifically in communities experiencing the most crime and violence, is that we are told that policing is the only solution. And since policing is the only solution presented, there is this reactive mindset to further increase police funding, which only increases salaries of police officers but does not decrease our experiences with violence or create safer communities. The safest communities never have more police officers, but rather access to more resources, including better jobs, schools, housing, and recreation, which make communities stronger.

Therefore, when politicians claim they want to ensure safer communities, why do they always default to increasing the number of police rather than invest in better housing and schools? Defund makes it clear that we should examine and scrutinize spending budgets. For example, in Paterson, an estimated $43 million goes to the police budget and recreation gets only $2 million.[87] Therefore, we argue that problems our kids are facing have to do with access to safe places to play and community space. At a minimum, Paterson can move a few million dollars from the police budget and put that toward recreation. This is just one example of solving problems that don't need police to ensure public safety and accountability.

CJS: *We know that crime and violence are real. What does an accountability framework look like within an abolitionist paradigm? In*

*other words, how do we replace archaic modes of policing and punish-
ment with restorative practices?*

ZI: This is part of the conservation we have with the eighth
graders in the healing circle, and it's fascinating that children
grasp these carceral logics more than some adults. For example, why would someone get suspended for violating the school's
dress code? The idea of taking away someone's opportunity to
learn because they are wearing crocs [shoes] is going to do more
violence than not adhering to an artificial dress code. As a society, we often associate accountability with corporeal punishment. If my bike was stolen, that violates me, but if the bike is
returned, I'm whole again; no further action needs to be taken.
To that end, if I don't get my bike back, I don't understand why
this violation means this person needs to spend the next several
years incarcerated. That doesn't make me whole; I'm still without
my bike. The more critical interrogation is: What has happened
in society to make this person feel the need to steal my bike? I
know these are hypotheticals, but defund highlights that when
violations happen in the community, they are connected back to
the lack of resources.

Prior to defund, policing and mass incarceration were perceived as these disconnected issues. Now, folks are making connections surrounding the disproportionate rates of Black boys
and girls expelled from school or why there are over three hundred missing Black women and girls that are not being reported
on news programs.

Finally, defund forces us to have deeper conversations about
the failures of this system. It begs the question of why we continue to pay people, and increase their pay, in the form of police,
courts, and prisons when we could use that money alternatively.
Our goal is to keep learning and producing alternatives to eradicate carceral logics and achieve defund logics.

CJS: *I appreciate that you brought up Black women and girls who have gone missing. Typically, marches, protests, and other sort of "boots on the ground" work happens when it is Black men who are shot or killed by police. Yet, we continue to see a lack of media coverage of Black women and trans folks who are brutalized or killed by law enforcement and others. Why do you think Black women, women of color, and trans folks receive less attention?*

ZI: Despite the number of viral videos or hashtags, it is a drop in the bucket in comparison to how many people are killed by police each year. Whether it is Black men or women, it is increasingly difficult to try to get any type of coverage. Sadly, we rely on videos going viral to be taken seriously and recognized. Yet, a person deserves justice with or without video evidence, and specifically Black women and trans folks who are ignored. #SayHerName was created to intentionally center Black women and trans folks because that conversation was not happening.[88] I believe, or want to believe, that a slow shift is happening. Ultimately, viral videos are used to verify a person's humanity.

CJS: *Speaking of "going viral," the Paterson police have done so on several occasions. For example, Roger Then and Ruben McAusland recorded themselves beating a man handcuffed to a hospital bed, and Jameek Lowery died under suspicious circumstances while in police custody.[89] Are these cases of the "few bad apples" analogy, or is this indicative of system-wide violence?*

ZI: Often, these incidents are presented as examples of the "bad apple" analogy and argue most cops are "good." Those arguments are always moot; because that person just brutalized or murdered someone. Police hold a monopoly on violence, and that makes them dangerous as an institution. If "good" people are in positions in which violence is the default, with impunity, that is a failing system. The ability to shoot to kill and be given special protections such as qualified immunity, which prevents any sort of true mediation of justice and accountability, must be dissolved.[90]

There is this myth that law enforcement is a "Superman" character that is infallible. Therefore, investigations, internal affairs reports, and grand juries go nowhere. Ultimately, cops are an occupying force in our communities. Further, police and police unions have a lot of political power, which is often wielded whenever any sort of accountability is implemented. They mobilize their constituents, highlighting how local governments such as mayors and city council representatives are afraid of political backlash. Therefore, if no one can hold police accountable, the next step is for them not to exist at all—which is not a radical idea. Elected officials are constantly reelected or replaced by voters. Yet the community cannot vote out the "bad" cop. Even the process to remove a single police officer is opaque, tedious, and prolonged. The best solution is abolition.

CJS: *Earlier, I mentioned how I learned about your work through social media—and you have a substantial presence, with over 145,000 Twitter followers and 38,000 Instagram followers.[91] Why do you think social media is important, if at all, to organizing, strategizing, and building coalitions in the community?*

ZI: Young millennials and Generation Z are growing up communicating in these sorts of digital spaces like TikTok and Instagram, learning about body shaming, racism, and worldly issues like the fight for Palestinian liberation. All these children are part of the Trayvon generation, seeing Black and Brown people killed,[92] which informs and impacts their mental health. Many are frustrated and angry but using this to build community.

I think about my own experiences with racism in college, feeling isolated and powerless; because these digital platforms didn't exist in the way they do now. Social media allows us to connect with others' experiences and realize that the pain and hopelessness is not isolated. From here, we build with each other across the country and the globe. We started to see the use of hashtags to identify various issues.[93] These platforms create community by allowing folks to see what others are doing, and vice versa, and most online organizing could not even be fathomed fifteen years ago. Now, we can "slide into the DMs [direct messages]" and discuss strategy through social media.

CJS: *On social media, you consistently post about mental health and self-care. Why are these important to organizing and strategy? What are some tips you can share on how you find balance between health and work? Finally, moving forward, what does sustainable activism look like in this new era?*

ZI: In 2020, I started going to therapy. I remember how scary the beginning of the pandemic was, and how we went from normal to isolation. I was afraid for myself and the folks doing mutual aid as we were outside everyday hearing about folks passing away from the virus.

Early on, there was a lot of varying information about transmissions and ways to protect oneself. I knew our work was putting us at a higher risk. At night, I would lay in bed and had to reconcile the fact I could get the virus, which could make me sick or kill me. This was before George Floyd's murder [by Minneapolis police]. After his death, I began getting phone calls to come down [to Minneapolis] to support the movement that was growing, which added more stress because I began to travel amidst a deadly pandemic. It was then that I realized I needed to start seeing a therapist to talk through my feelings. I wish everyone had access to this sort of care. I recognized I needed to do things for myself like go on walks, bicycle rides, and talk to friends as part of my self-care. Also, I had to learn and understand that "No" is a complete sentence. Individuals, especially organizers, do not need to solve all problems nor have the capacity to support everybody. My role as an organizer is to empower those around me to also solve issues. Learning to say no has been refreshing.

Finally, community organizers must be ready to shift mobi-
lization efforts and have an action plan of how to educate and
empower. No movement should ever rely on one person. If something happened to me, movement-building does not stop. That
is why we share tasks. If I'm the person who oversees making
fliers, it should never just be me doing this work, but I'm training and working with others, sharing my skills, experiences, and
resources. This is what makes organizations bigger, better, and
stronger. Movements are never about the individual; it's about us.
There is no single winner, but all of us winning, and that's how
we sustain "community is a verb."

CHAPTER 4

"Those Who Can, Must!"
with Olayemi Olurin

Olayemi Olurin is a lawyer, political commentator, and social media influencer who reports on issues related to the criminal legal system, both in New York City and across the United States. Our discussion touches upon several topics that are both directly and indirectly related to the broader defund movement.

First, we talk about what it means to be a public defender in New York City, including how the public perceives them and the specific work in which she engages on the part of her clients, both inside and outside of the courtroom. Here, Ms. Olurin interrogates the various methods used in demanding justice such as advocacy and the use of social media. Second, our conversation examines the concept of "copaganda"—discourses at the society level that serve to uphold and normalize violent policing practices. Ms. Olurin is candid that defund, as a movement, is crucial to efforts to combat poverty.

Next, we talk about New York City city's largest jail, Rikers Island, the impact of the election of Mayor Eric Adams on the city's approach to policing, and the negative focus on drill music by police and public officials as a scapegoat for societal problems. Lastly, we touch on the role of self-care and its importance to both the physical and mental well-being of those engaged in abolitionist struggle. Reckoning with the stakes contemporary political, social, and pop culture issues, Ms. Olurin provides a keen analysis of how defund can move us toward abolition.

* * *

CJS: *Who inspired you to pursue a career in law and become a public defender? Often, this career path is scrutinized by the public, either as defending guilty people or as not caring about those you defend.*

OO: It is a frustrating experience. But, coming from Nassau, The Bahamas, my grammy [grandmother] always told me that I was going to be a lawyer. That influenced my decision to come to America and pursue law.

In college I minored in African American studies and earned a certificate in law, justice, and culture as well as in women and gender studies. My thesis, called "Colored Bodies Matter: The Relationship between Our Bodies and Power," examined how the law is set up to inherently dehumanize Black bodies by keeping them in jail. At first, I questioned if I wanted to be a "Black" lawyer, and if it was going to be simply symbolic of "Black excellence" that did nothing for the community. However, I wanted to use my law degree to help protect people from laws that control every aspect of life, and that is why I became a public defender.

To your second point, public defenders get blamed for everything that is wrong with the legal system. It is a thankless job because many, especially peers, assume public defenders are less qualified, don't make as much money, and are not "real" lawyers. On the contrary, The Legal Aid Society, my employer, is very competitive.[94] Conversely, community members might not trust, and speak down to, public defenders. However, I am reminded, people are frustrated when they get caught up in the [legal] system because it puts them in terrible positions.

CJS: *Considering that you are not from the United States, what does it mean to be a Black immigrant woman practicing in the legal field? How has your lived experiences informed your law career?*

OO: It has everything to do with my resident status. I can tell people until I'm blue in the face that I'm an immigrant, but most people just see a Black woman and assume I'm American. The reality is, my immigrant status comes before anything; because there are many restrictions. Yet, in other ways, being an immigrant has forged positive relationships with clients, especially working with Caribbean migrants in New York City. My colleagues literally don't understand their clients' dialects, whereas I do. And because of my own status, I know immigration law better than the average public defender.

My immigrant experience allows me to anticipate a lot of questions to help clients navigate the system. Some colleagues were upset with my holistic approach, claiming that was not our job. But immigration is important. Beyond that, being a young Black woman with a hyper-sexualized body type creates bullshit I must confront. Often, I think about how some of my colleagues interact with me and consider how they see clients in a dehumanizing and disrespectful way.

CJS: *During the summer 2020 uprisings, you were at protest sites as a legal observer. By now, we have seen the numerous recordings of police brutality at these events. Can you share what the energy and climate was like for activists and law enforcement responses?*

OO: I'm not somebody who only champions peaceful protests. With that said, the summer 2020 protests were peaceful. Each time, NYPD [New York Police Department] would stand across the street and wait until nightfall, then, under the cover of darkness, run into crowds and start a commotion by hitting somebody to create the appearance of violence. And this would be justification to arrest people. Police would escalate violence by cutting demonstrators off and block them from crossing a bridge and then wait until it was "curfew," which is made up by the state, to justify inflicting harm.

I can only recall one protest where I saw an individual take a skateboard and hit parked cars. The larger group swarmed this person and forced them to stop because of this notion of remaining peaceful as part of the strategy being used by the collective group. I remember tweeting out about this; because as a lawyer, I'm a cog in the system. I recognize and do not consider myself a revolutionary, because I *literally* work within the system. Yet I constantly remind folks that arrests occur, and as a defense attorney, I want to avoid that for you. However, to be revolutionary and use tactics of resistance, you must assume those risks.

Further, as a legal observer, I'm not supposed to say anything, but I have witnessed arguments between protesters, especially surrounding various actions. For example, a small group of protesters were doing something, and another group came running over like, "Stop, you are going to cause the police to come," and someone responded, "Stop policing how we protest." And I get it. We all want peace, but that is not always the right strategy. On the one hand, various tactics outside of peaceful protest are going to draw negative consequences. On the other hand, true resistance isn't meant to be comfortable. Protests are not supposed to be done within the confines of nicety. The reason peace is echoed so loudly is to not disrupt the system.

Who is anybody to tell someone else how to resist oppression? We are all taking risks that could be life changing. There is no "right" or "wrong," but rather just preferences of strategy. In the end, we are all potentially sacrificing our lives.

CJS: *And violence can be transgressive.*

OO: Violence is celebrated as revolutionary for everybody but Black folks. There is no context in America when White folks' response to injustice peacefully. Yet for Black folks it must be peaceful and nonviolent, even in the wake of extreme violence.

Therefore, how can I or anybody, in good faith, tell Black people, or anyone fighting against oppression, that you can't break property or be mad. People are being murdered in the street and we see this rush to protect property, which is given higher value than Black lives. The argument to defend property is always from outsiders, not the community. Perhaps the community doesn't feel the same connection to the banks and businesses that don't employ them or loan them money.

CJS: *In the article "Law and Order Taught Americans to Root for the Police," published in* Teen Vogue, *you write, "We're taught to fear and dislike the people caught in the crossfire of the criminal legal system, rather than to fear the system that inflicts pain on them."*[95] *This passage resonates because it highlights the degree of society's indoctrination surrounding our criminal legal system—from media representations of law enforcement to childhood games like "cops and robbers." Could you elaborate on your statement and how it manifests every day in courtrooms?*

OO: Recently, my niece called and asked if I was a prosecutor, and I told her I was a defense attorney. She responded, "You represent the bad guys?" I reminded her, "I'm on the good side."

One of the first things that kids learn is copaganda.[96] Shows like *Paw Patrol* and *Power Puff Girls* are all about police. All of this creates an environment where anyone opposite of the police is viewed as the villain, regardless of their story arc. This translates to real life as there is no presumption of innocence. I'm frequently asked how I sleep at night representing guilty people; because copaganda is where folks' analysis starts. Yet, when you look at the circumstances of the people within the criminal system, it is made up of poor folks.

While there is this presumption of innocence, the prosecutor and judge are making bail determinations based on allegations, not convictions, and I've witnessed how it can take seconds to put somebody in jail but forever to get them out. The reason why this is allowed to happen is because people don't have a problem with, or fully understand, the way the system operates, as many are complicit in what they are told by media, police, and courts.

Pretrial detainees are shipped off to Rikers Island, which is comprised of nearly 90 percent Black and Latinx folks.[97] To add insult, this penal colony is given an absurd amount of money to operate because of the indoctrination of the criminal legal system that simply says, "Fuck them, it doesn't matter what happens."[98]

CJS: *We are trained to see someone being pulled over or detained in the subway as having done something wrong.*

OO: The question begs: *Who* is being detained?

As a woman, I'm conscious of my surroundings, and the police are included in this awareness. If I am in majority-Black neighborhoods, I fully understand how my presence in that space is perceived by law enforcement differently than if I'm in a courtroom because of how race is intrinsically connected to perceptions of crime. However, it is also a class analysis linked to opinions of "professionalism" and attire, which sees a blazer, skirt, and heels as qualified and sneakers, jeans, and jacket as criminal.

These presumptions translate into the way folks are discussed in the criminal system. The moment a person is put in jail, their name is no longer used but rather referred to by a docket number. Even media reporting on someone dying in jail uses phrases like "inmate died," stripping them of humanity. Their name, background, or other details don't matter; it really becomes a "fuck them" situation, and that is because of how America heavily propagandized law enforcement, right down to *Paw Patrol.*

CJS: *Since 2020, defund and abolition have become part of mainstream lexicon, and various groups from the left, center, and right have either supported, been confused, or admonished the terms. Do* *you see defund as a moment or a movement, and are these terms synonymous, complimentary, dichotomous, or something else?*

OO: Defund is a movement. It is the manifestation of a movement catching steam. Abolition has been the long-term goal, beginning with the abolition of slavery. Defund is a culmination of people, particularly moderates, coming to terms with this system. Folks have all sorts of criticisms of defund as a deliberate tactic, because if defund was impossible or not a threat to the status quo, there wouldn't be daily op-eds and politicians talking about it.

Defund has teeth. I was watching *Bel-Air,*[99] and the character "Uncle Phil" is running for district attorney and is asked about his position on defund. It highlights how important defund has become to the national conversation. It is a standard inquiry, even in a fictious drama. The reason it is talked about so much is that the power structure wants to convince us it is impossible and to abandon the idea. Yet, defund is very possible. It is probably the most plausible thing that could happen in the short term.

Often, movement objectives are not always concrete, and the power structure throws up their hands and feign ignorance on how to do it. Defund is not that. This is one of those areas that elected officials can play a pronounced role in making effective change since they control budgets. And they know *we know* they can do it, because we see them cut budgets on everything else. This is a promising movement, and stakeholders invested in the status quo are terrified. Otherwise, defund would not be discussed. If defund was truly irrelevant, no breath would be wasted on it.

The statement "People don't support defund" is a strawman argument. History has shown that most forms of resistance begin with minority support. Part of movement-building is winning over the majority over time. Most of America approved of slavery, and the same politicians who now claim they are fighting for prison reform were the ones creating policies that led to the prison industrial complex. Defund, at its inception, is a policy demand, with room to expand. Changes rarely happen overnight, in sweeping ways, so we can't be discouraged by detractors in the moment.

I read scholars and revolutionary activists who do this work until their last breath. We can't quantify successes based on some silly measurement in the moment. James Baldwin worked his entire life toward freedom. Angela Davis continues to do the work. More recently, Mariame Kaba has written two books[100] in the last year and shows no signs of stopping; because this work is a lifelong fight. In college, I read Angela Davis's book *Are Prisons Obsolete?*[101] It became a life-changing journey of social consciousness. Because we are not taught or exposed to alternatives to prisons; we see these institutions as innate, and to get rid of them is posited as crazy. Finally, an important factor is that most people who end up in prison are financially broke. However, the "true crime" genre tries to convince us that these people are just inherently bad and if that's the case, there is nothing that can be done and locking them up makes sense.

CJS: *Do you approach your career from an abolitionist framework? If so, what does abolition look like within the halls of justice, and how do we abolish police, courts, and prisons while ensuring public safety?*

OO: In short, yes, and my job extends beyond the courtroom. As an attorney, you must play within the confines of the system, but the way I feel about the system informs my activism.

I am an outlier, as other public defenders are proponents of the criminal legal system. The reality is many people working in this system are invested in the system. I diverge from this and truly believe that we need to rid this system. Therefore, I operate by letting my clients know that the system is fucked up. What they did or did not do is completely immaterial to me. The

injustice in and of itself is the society that puts people in the position to have to meet me.

The real crime is poverty. Anybody I represent is dirt poor. I
cannot raise a dog on my salary and have no disposable income.
Yet, I would still not qualify for my own services. I very much
consider myself broke *but not* impoverished. For people to qualify for my services and be represented by a public defender, you
must have almost nothing. No income or money. And that's most
people in the system.[102]

Also, there are fines and fees associated with every crime. So
the court recognizes that individuals who qualify for my services have no money but insists on imposing monetary penalties,
which if not paid add further legal consequences. Beyond this,
while in jail, individuals experience violence, sexual assault, and
other forms of psychological and physical trauma, which is then
brought back into the community to expose others to these trau-
matic experiences indirectly.

When you look at the system through this perspective, the in-
nocence-or-guilt question is moot. My duty is to serve my client
to the best of my ability. But how can I alleviate the collateral
consequences? Because the harm of the criminal legal system
goes beyond simply being in a jail. Rather, it leaves many with
a criminal conviction, which has further consequences such as
the ability to find a job, housing, and other social resources. All
of this together creates cycles of sociological and psychological
violence in communities.

For perspective, I come from a Black country, Nassau, The
Bahamas. My country is one of the most expensive by cost of
living in the world, and our minimum wage is $5.25, which is
equal to the US dollar.[103] Therefore, I know a lot of poor people,
but we don't have the same social issues because we are not oppressed in the same way by our government. Simply put, crime
is not inherent to race but how certain groups are oppressed and
monitored closely.

Ultimately, my abolitionist framework is to figure out how to combat the system at every step as I advocate for my clients, particularly beyond what happens in the courtroom. This informs my recognition that just being a day-to-day attorney is insufficient, and doing outward-facing advocacy and education informs my abolitionist praxis.

CJS: *You have been active in the Close Rikers Campaign.*[104] *In 2019, the New York City Council voted to shut down the penal colony. However, the compromise was to build four new borough jails.*[105] *How does this reform effort exacerbate carceral logics and undermine defund?*

OO: The Department of Corrections has an annual budget of over a billion dollars.[106] Therefore, we know it is not an issue of funding. Rikers Island was opened in 1932, and some argue that the jail is simply old. However, this reductionist view ignores that the problem is the system, not the location. Rikers Island was not built on some sort of special "demon" soil. Therefore, the same issues of violence, trauma, and locking up poor people will continue in the new jails.

There is also no sense of urgency on behalf of the state to close this facility, which has unsanitary conditions, unsafe environments, and people dying.[107] Judges and prosecutors are very aware of the situation at Rikers and consistently ignore those alarms because individuals are still sent. The reality is, the actors who uphold the system don't give a fuck about these people.

CJS: *In a since-deleted tweet, the @NYPDnews account posted an image of officers proudly displaying the recovery of roughly $1,800 of stolen pampers and toiletry items. There was immediate social media backlash. What can you tell us about this sort of posturing from the police? It seems as if the idea of stealing supplies that individuals need to survive is the very reason why "defund the police" exists.*

OO: The system is bullshit. The NYPD deleted the tweet, but did they drop the case? If folks reading this are outraged by police doing fucked up shit like charging poor people with a crime for stealing basic needs, or if you were outraged by the murder of George Floyd, then you should be in a permanent state of outrage. Police impose their will at every turn and use lethal force every chance they get. Police kill someone every day, and that's not hyperbole.[108]

CJS: *Eric Adams was elected the 110th mayor of New York City in November 2021. Yet his victory seems to reflect a warped sense of identity politics. Yes, he is a Black man, but his positions, specifically on criminal justice, evoke the "broken windows" and "tough on crime" era.[109] Do you think he would have been elected if he was anything other than a Black man?*

OO: Yes and no. Eric Adams was elected because he gives "White"—meaning his viewpoints, as a Black man, appeal to Whites moderates. The baseline for White Democrats is status quo diversity initiatives, which is having the presence of someone different but nothing changing. His Blackness certainly secured many Black votes, too, because Black folks have been indoctrinated with the same bullshit that White moderates adhere to.

Adams is the definition of status quo Negro who won't rock the boat. He became the answer for folks in power who were shook to the core after summer 2020. It reminds me of Derrick Bell, a critical race theorist, who elaborates that anytime a Black person enters White America, there is an opportunity to sell out and become White supremacy's token if you legitimize its talking points.[110] Race is one of those rare instances that Black folks are considered an expert. So if you are parroting White supremacy on how to deal with crime, violence, and public safety, you are simply rubber-stamping an entrenched and wrong system.

Further, the problem with racism in the criminal system is that it is positioned as Democrat versus Republican. The former projected as the "do-gooders" and the latter as "evil." The reality is both parties are doing the same thing. New York City is overwhelmingly Democrat-elected officials, yet this progressive metropolis has a notoriously evil criminal legal system, culminating in Rikers Island.

New York literally elected a cop in the wake of the largest civil rights movement in US history and millions of people across the globe calling for "defund the police."[111] This is on top of the fact that the NYPD has police brutality cases every single day.[112] And the Democrats are like, "Let's elect a fucking cop."

CJS: *In February 2022, Eric Adams attacked drill music, blaming crime on this subgenre of hip hop. He was swiftly criticized and then met with some NYC-based rappers.*[113] *Why do you think Adams used drill as his scapegoat, and what are your thoughts on his meeting with artists?*

OO: That was performative bullshit. I wish those young men would have told him no. I understand it is hard to get your foot in the door and have that opportunity, but sometimes you've got to tell someone to fuck off. The meeting was nothing more than an appeal to White folks that reinforced their opinions about hip hop, youth, and Black culture, because there are many celebrated outlets that express violence, like video games and film, but we don't see Adams trying to ban video game programmers or Netflix. These sorts of press conferences are only reserved for Black culture. Adams is not genuine but rather a fearmonger about crime—which is an exaggeration because it is not reflective of the actual data.[114] Further, anyone who cares about public safety would critically assess the causes of crime and violence, which is poverty.

On top of this, it should not cost this much to live in this city, as the stratification of wealth is disgusting. It is not drill music inflicting harm but rather a system that has continuously ignored communities, and the only response is *more cops.* The drill scene is art imitating life. They are rapping about poverty, violence, and police brutality. Every time these young artists are arrested or Adams wants to ban the music, it reinforces all the societal issues they are discussing in their music that continue to be ignored and why defund resonates so soundly.

CJS: *Why do you think social media is an important tool for organizing and building community?*

OO: A broad following gives power in a way that helps accomplish the kind of change we want to see because it can put a spotlight on injustice. We can't be naive and think we are going to change the hearts and minds of everyone, but we can use whatever power is available to combat their stances.

My Twitter following happened organically, as I did not set out to be Twitter famous. I was minding my own business, but then [New York governor Andrew] Cuomo tried to fuck up bail reform.[115] Legal Aid [Society] encouraged us to tweet about this to express our dissatisfaction with the plan. In doing so, I called out a racist school segregationist who was running for public office. After this, a racist White man reposted pictures of me from my birthday, attempting to troll me by writing, "If you need to see somebody who uses their body to get the job." He thought it was a "gotcha" moment, but *I* posted these pictures. How is he going to try and body-shame me with something I voluntarily shared on social media?

Regardless, his tweet made me the subject of #LawTwitter for a day, which was around the time of George Floyd's murder. Soon thereafter, I had a high-profile police-brutality case. Between all these events, I started to see the number of followers continue to rise, and next thing I know, I had thousands of followers, which opened more doors and led to political commentary and other opportunities that are important to bring attention to the criminal system.

Having this platform gives me the ability to bring attention to cases, even if I'm not directly involved. However, I'm most proud of getting a couple prosecutors fired by exposing their racism and bias. Now, even politicians, such as AOC [US Representative Alexandra Ocasio-Cortez] are following and listening to me. I can put ideas forth and create a discourse, which might seem "radical" today but become accepted tomorrow. But that does not happen without making information available.

CJS: *Finally, what is the role of self-care? More specifically, what are strategies or tips to find the balance between your physical and mental health and the work you do?*

OO: The work is emotionally draining. There is a lot of secondhand or adjacent trauma, and I'm not going to say it doesn't impact me. I go to court at night and feel things differently.

My self-care is that I'm in therapy, talk to friends, and have community to share space and time with. I have colleagues who I vent to, and vice versa; it becomes a reciprocal form of care. Also, I read a lot, which helps reframe my perspectives, especially about things that get me upset. As much as having a social media platform gives power, people are constantly saying stupid shit in the comments or sending death threats. Reading is comforting because it reminds me that I am not the first person to have these experiences.

I'll end how I started. I'm from the tiny island of Nassau, The Bahamas, and people close to me are concerned about my safety. And I'm not foolish. I understand the risk involved with having a platform. However, my philosophy is that those who can, *must!* If I can do these things, I'm going to do what I can because it is necessary to use your voice, fight for liberation, and abolish this system.

CHAPTER 5

"Pragmatic Abolitionism"
with Jonathan Ilan

Jonathan Ilan is an assistant professor in criminology at Sutherland School of Law, University College Dublin.[116] His research interests include ethnographic methodology, hip hop, and cultural criminology. His scholarship contends with poverty, youth, crime, and the "cool," exploring representation, authenticity, and forms of inclusion and exclusion within street culture.[117] Furthermore, he has published on UK drill music and how this subgenre of hip hop is criminalized by authorities through their use of lyrics and music videos as evidence of violence and crime.[118]

In our conversation, we discuss how the murder of George Floyd by Minneapolis police was experienced in Europe, the relationship between colonialism and police violence on both sides of the Atlantic, and the nuances of abolition not only as an ideological platform but as praxis. To do this, we consider how colonialism and post-colonialism continue to shape race and stratification, specifically their monopoly on the use of violence. From here, we examine in depth the drill scene as a musical form, illustrating the interconnected bonds that Black music has as both resistance and defiance in the wake of social movements. Finally, we theorize abolition in two different ways: as a "light switch" and as a "pragmatic" approach. The former is concerned with the immediate needs and short-term goals of an abolitionist praxis, while the latter grapples with long-term visions of abolition. In this conversation, we recognize that both forms of abolition are vital to sustaining the struggle to transform our world.

*   *   *

CJS: *In the wake of George Floyd's murder, what was the overall feeling in Europe, specifically in London?*

JI: I had conversations with colleagues, and we had this feeling of déjà vu. Each time it brings this crushing feeling, but initially it didn't have the sense that it was necessarily different. Yet we know the global impact this murder had, which brought about this idea of "enough is enough." Perhaps [the COVID-19 pandemic] presented a model that things must get done.

When tragedies happen in America, the world watches. The gross level of violence in this case sparked [London's] Metropolitan Police and many legislators to tweet "Black Lives Matter" solidarity messages.[119] The hypocrisy is that Rashan Charles and Edson Da Costa, both Black men, died while in Met custody.[120] Therefore, we see this connection between folks in the [United] States and in the UK fighting the same injustices as well as the disconnect of public officials saying this is a terrible event but only seeing it as an "American problem." This sort of cognitive dissonance highlights how racism goes unchecked in Europe. Yet, the historical precedent and context is that not only does racism exist in Europe, but it began here. Ultimately, government officials and corporations admonish racism when it is presented as an external issue.

CJS: *The phrase "Black lives matter" began trending across the globe in summer 2020 from places such as the United States to the United*

Kingdom to Seoul, South Korea.[121] *While the impetus for these demonstrations was George Floyd's murder, it felt as if communities were connecting this death to local issues as well, adding a layer of nuance.*

JI: The United States is the center of cultural hegemony. Therefore, issues resonate and reverberate globally, creating this call for solidarity to make change and address inequality. In the initial days of protest in London, people were making connections with campaigns and issues that were already happening. Various struggles that were brewing for decades, that had sparks, were able to become explosive after Mr. Floyd's death.

Additionally, the pandemic played an interesting role. For years, governments around the world did nothing, but this contagious virus generated a massive response to save lives and stop the spread. This is not to say that all governments handled the virus in the best way, but we saw things, with debate, get done. This became important to the movement because people realized that governments could be efficient and these warring political parties could come together and pass legislation or make concessions for the greater good of society. The movement saw this as an opportunity to exploit that, with good reason; to attempt to make substantial social change.

Lastly, isolation played a role as George Floyd's death gave folks a reason to go outside and demand justice. There was a bizarre sense of normalcy and a reprieve but also an empowering moment, as this movement was not only made up of people on the proverbial "left" but rather people of all political allegiances. Many saw this death as a moment of reflexivity to contend with police brutality and a public health crisis.

CJS: *I was struck by how demonstrations were being linked to global capitalism and White supremacist hegemony as statues and other symbols of White supremacy were torn down or destroyed. For example, the statue of Edward Colston, an English merchant and notorious slave trader for the Royal African Company, was thrown into Bristol*

Harbour.[122] *Do you think these connections and strategies are important to movements?*

JI: Yeah, these kinds of connections have been developing. For example, Oxford University's Rhodes Scholarship program, named after Cecil Rhodes—the founder of De Beers, a South African diamond mining company—has come under scrutiny in recent years. He was a vehement racist and imperialist who utilized various forms of violence and exploitation of Indigenous populations to accumulate his wealth. The "Rhodes Must Fall" movement advocated for the award to be renamed, the removal of his statue, and racial transformation at the university.[123]

There becomes a scaffolding of movements that layer on top of each other. For instance, while slavery is often posited as only happening in the Americas, modern Europe was built on the money generated through the slave trade. Europe can deflect much of this history because some of the worst aspects of colonialism "happened over there," referring to the Americas and Africa. Yet, regardless of distance, the money flowed into Europe and built hospitals, universities, and museums. Most importantly, it made many people very wealthy.

As an Irish person living in London, I see how British colonial history is insufficiently taught. Therefore, many people are just not aware of how this trauma informs contemporary colonial and post-colonial relationships. When these associations are recognized and acknowledged, the connections you posed are much easier to understand—the relationship from the slave trade to summer 2020.

CJS: *The World Cup is a prime example of post-colonialism. European nations with multiracial teams did not happen organically or through a sense of altruism but rather tied to those histories of violence and imperialism.*

Why do you think the term "defund" caught on in 2020 as a way of building solidarity frameworks?

JI: Interestingly, in England, the Conservative Party had already begun cutting police funding prior to the defund movement because of austerity spending. Nevertheless, I show students charts of American cities' bloated police budgets. In Europe, there is slightly more parity as there is a more robust welfare state. While I agree with defund, particularly as a smart strategy, I'm not sure if the phrase as a policy initiative resonates in the same way here. I assume there could always be more cuts, but our government is already doing it—however, not with the same motivations.

In the states, "defund" has a particular strength. On the one hand, a liberal can look at the term and say they want a model that is more closely aligned to European nations. On the other hand, an abolitionist can use the term to advocate eradicating police completely. Therefore, in terms of movement building, having a concept with broad appeal allows for more people to get behind the message.

"Defund" cuts through the jargon that many reformers and radicals alike debate. Often, phrases are abstract and hard to grasp, but "defund" provides an achievable goal, through policy, for reformers but also creates a guide to less state-violence in the form of surveillance and police for the abolitionists. In the end, everyone wants public safety, but how to get there is where it gets hazy. In sum, defund gives a starting point.

CJS: *Part of the defund campaign is disentangling the idea that police equal public safety, as there are various examples of police exacerbating social problems. For example, in New York City, police would use condoms as probable cause for arrest, which disproportionately targeted youth LGBTQIA+ folks of color, creating public health risks as sex workers and others stopped carrying condoms, increasing risk of sexual disease transmission.*[124]

JI: Society often connects policing to the people who wear the blue shirts. The reality is, "policing" is about keeping an eye out and making sure everything is okay. I know it might fringe on semantics, but even if formal police are abolished—which many people can't fathom—there will be some form of "policing" per se. The problem is the way in which "policing" has been institutionalized in the United States. In Ireland and England, most police do not carry guns. This is not to say they don't commit police brutality, but there is something very "American" about a person policing with a gun that makes the propensity for violence rise dramatically.

CJS: *In the United States, law enforcement responses to progressive and leftist movements, in comparison to conservative and far-right demonstrations, are much more vicious. Do you see these same distinctions in Europe?*

JI: There is variation within Europe, but there are certainly far-right ideologies entangled within police and military. In the UK, police have been used as strikebreakers as well as to monitor leftist movements, while right-wing causes went under the radar. Interestingly, in the age of "global terror," policing has designed and implemented systems to catch early radicalization and extremism, which has had an unintended consequence of catching people on the far right.

The pandemic has spawned several anti-vaccination protests. Subsequently, police have been deployed, and some have caught the virus and died. Therefore, it creates a situation where individual agents might be more politically aligned with these right-wing protesters against COVID protocols, but then exposed to the virus, making them question the aims of these anti-vax demonstrations. Maybe I'm an eternal optimist, but seeing how this virus is harming everyone, regardless of race, class, or political persuasion, it might be a moment of coming together.

CJS: *As a scholar of street culture, particularly hip hop music, can you contextualize the drill scene and its relationship to resistance and defiance?*

JI: Drill originated in Chicago in the early 2010s at a moment of horrific gun violence, which is pervasive in the lyrics and the kinds of activities the artists are speaking about.[125] The scene also begins during the proliferation of social media, and many artists use these platforms to promote their art but also convey and send shots [insults] to other youth and opposing cliques and gangs.[126]

The intimacy with violence and street culture, particularly surrounding marginality, contextualizes many of the drill artists' experiences. For example, Chief Keef, a native of South Side Chicago, is one of the earliest kinds of drill success stories becoming popular through a viral music video.[127] This unfiltered sound set the genre apart and reinvigorated notions of authenticity within hip hop culture.

From here, drill resonated in London and then back to the States, specifically Brooklyn, New York, as this rejection of social conventions. However, drill is not rebel music, as many of the themes are based in violence but also accumulation of wealth. In fact, I would argue, drill in many ways comfortably resonates within a late-capitalism paradigm—the idea of "get rich or die tryin.'"[128] Yet, it is still a layered narrative because it's calling for the enrichment of the most deeply marginalized poor, to strive for luxury.

However, there is still this sense that life is cheap and cut short because of the violence endured, highlighting that at the core of the scene is tragedy and trauma. Moreover, there is a voyeurism happening, as traditional hip hop consumers, which is largely a middle-class non-Black demographic, have become the purchasers that generate the wealth the artists are attempting to achieve, as the artists navigate violence, poverty, and marginalization.

CJS: *Arguably the most famous drill artist is Pop Smoke. Born in Brooklyn, New York, to Jamaican and Panamanian parents, he was affiliated with the Crips street gang and had been justice impacted before recording his hit record "Welcome to the Party," released in April 2019. Tragically, on February 19, 2020, at age twenty, Pop Smoke was murdered in Los Angeles. However, his single "Dior," a reference to the high-end French luxury brand, which discusses the braggadocio lifestyle of wealth, women, and hyper-masculinity became the anthem of the summer 2020 protests. Why do you think drill music, specifically this song, was adopted by the movement, and how do you see drill connected to protest?*

JI: First, young people seeing friends die is something that is occurring in London as well. It highlights neocolonialism, which brings folks from around the globe from developing nations with this promise of making life better. Yet the reality is many are still ignored and endure suffering, even in these "lands of opportunity."

The second point about mental health is one of the things I like so much about your work: you find the positive amidst the tragedy. It is important that young folks who come from marginalized backgrounds have a language to speak. I'm saddened that drill is being criminalized as young folks are bearing their souls through the lyrics to unpack their pain. Yet those words are then used against them in court, and music videos are used as evidence to link artists to gangs and murder cases.[129]

Pop Smoke's career has made a lasting impact. You brought up Smoke's background, and I'm drawn to [sociologist] Paul Gilroy's work *The Black Atlantic*.[130] This connection of Caribbean origins in New York and Pop Smoke's records produced by East London producer 808Melo perfectly exemplifies Gilroy's argument of the Black Atlantic's expansiveness. To that end, it is interesting to think about why this song about shopping became the anthem of this movement at that moment.

Kendrick Lamar's "Alright" had been an anthem in previous years, with a deeper political message. Yet this moment was looking for something different. [Critical criminologist] Eleni Dimou and I wrote a piece, "Taking Pleasure Seriously: The Political Significance of Subcultural Practice."[131] We argue that those who see subcultural practice, such as hip hop, as decorative or as a distraction to the "real" issues miss the point. Often it is these practices that bring people together, in fellowship, and feel energized. "Dior" is a top-notch party tune that is full of this kind of vitality. Protests and marches are a tiresome experience as your feet begin to hurt, the evenings cool off, and long stretches can be, frankly, boring. To have a song that brings a high level of energy can form solidarity. That sort of organic solidarity that [sociologist Émile] Durkheim discussed.[132] This idea of "I actually *feel* part of the movement," with the people around you.

In 2010, rising university fees sparked demonstrations throughout London.[133] At that time a grime song, "Pow," by Lethal Bizzle, became a celebrated anthem at many rallies. Ironically, the song had been banned from some nightclubs because, allegedly, crowds would create a ruckus. Songs like "Pow" and "Dior" are important for social movements because they highlight that movements don't exist solely as academic discourse but are very much reliant on public intellectuals and various art forms. Pop [Smoke] certainly did not set out to be the anthem of a movement, but the energy he put into that record provides a platform for this community folks were searching for.

CJS: *The beat, cadence, and Pop Smoke's deep voice drives that energy, to the point that I'm not sure if the lyrics mattered in that moment. The song became a rallying cry, highlighting that for something to be revolutionary it does not need to be limited to a certain set of ideas. In other words, it was less about what he said but rather how he said it.*

JI: Exactly. That is my point about resistance versus defiance: it does not have to be this tight articulation of ideas. Often, resistance is posited as needing a ten-point plan for "reducing police violence." Yet, defiance does not have these guidelines. Pop Smoke is speaking, from a Marxist perspective, as someone coming from the lumpenproletariat, who are written about but often looked down upon. The idea of artists narrating their lives from the realities of violence and aspirations of wealth summarizes our relation to capitalism.

CJS: *How does the "cool" show up in defund? In particular, how have we seen street culture influence and become tethered to social movements?*

JI: There is this amazing interview of N.W.A. from the late '80s or early '90s on the Arsenio Hall [talk]show, and the group critiques Black Power and Free South Africa, taking an apolitical position.[134] The group was adhering to strict cultural posturing that politics is not part of the identity of hip hop.

Meanwhile, their classic song "Fuck the Police" is highly political—I could argue, more political than some politically intended songs of the era—highlighting my point about defiance, which is about rejection of any sort of mainstream identity because it was "uncool." Yet, how can a group that discusses police brutality and fighting cops be seen as anything but inherently political?

Simultaneously, there is something provocative about N.W.A.'s statements. In that moment, the group is not just agitating White middle-class America but also the Black community, which sees these statements as ignorant. N.W.A. did not aesthetically appeal to the respectability politics of previous Black generations. Ultimately, the notion of the "cool" has shifted in the last thirty years. Today, political engagement with BLM and defund no longer has a specific dress code or particular theoretical framework. That is why songs like "Dior," which are not written with political motivation, can still become anthems for movements.

To that end, it is important to highlight the symbiosis between hip hop and American incarceration, which disproportionately impacts low-income young Black men. However, this "American exceptionalism" is not unique, as Britain has a disproportionate amount of people of color in prison. In fact, England and Wales are disproportionately worse than America. David Lammy, a member of parliament, was commissioned by the government to examine how Black people and ethnic minorities are treated within the criminal justice system, which reflects this disparity.[135] While the UK does not see the same volume of people going into our prisons as in America, there are other sorts of crossovers, such as the move to longer sentences, which reflects a more American punitive system.

CJS: *Adding to the increase of incarceration is the widespread use of criminal surveillance, such as ankle monitors and facial recognition software, which has been shown to be racially biased and unreliable.[136] How do you see this technology further criminalize and marginalize already-vulnerable populations?*

JI: There is a serious issue with a lot of algorithms and software packages; because they are only as good as the data that is being put into them. We must question where this information is coming from and the preexisting bias within intelligence agencies.

Technology is given a faux objectivity whenever there is this "science-ish" or "data-ish" hue to it. The late great [sociologist] Jock Young pointed out the insanity of criminological mathematical equations that produce all types of inequalities.[137] Facial-recognition software is the latest iteration of previous forms of surveillance, such as "you match the description" type of reports. Now we are seeing this classic racist trope being digitized, which leads to the "usual suspects."

Further, not to sound too provocative, but I think this is a big issue, and an especially scary debate for abolitionists—because what replaces the technology? Of course we should be putting humanity first, but we see how social conflict is outsourced to machines, computers, and algorithms to solve the problems.

CJS: *I think about this tension with technology. For example, my iPhone uses facial recognition. I can recognize the problematic issues with this technology but, at the same time, appreciate the convenience it has for my personal use.*

JI: Right, and this becomes a dilemma within abolitionist frameworks. This sort of "light switch" abolition has the potential to expand problems, not solve them. It goes back to my earlier comments about police. We can agree that the traditional blue-shirt police are problematic, but even if we get rid of them, I imagine some sort of policing would still replace it to ensure public safety.

The larger discussion about surveillance capitalism and who owns the data and digital rights to this information is important, but I think there is a real need for abolitionists to have these difficult conversations, because I fear that sometimes we risk putting the cart in front of the horse. There are many factors because of the histories of inequality, marginalization, trauma, and exploitation that need to be sorted out that simply eradicating a system does not resolve. Therefore, I'm deeply committed to abolitionist changes, but I am also cautious.

CJS: *As an abolitionist, something that is inspiring is the idea that abolition creates space for reimagining society. All the conflicts that you bring up need to be simultaneously addressed as we eliminate frameworks of inequality and exploitation.*

I would argue for a "pragmatic abolitionism," which juxtaposes the "light switch" model. I think both should happen. For example, when thinking about prison abolition, the "light switch" model should be used to end practices such as pretrial detainment, solitary confinement, and capital punishment. Conversely, while I am committed to the closure of jails and prisons on a macro level, there are community tensions that need to be addressed in tandem with this struggle for prison abolition.

For instance, I think of the teenage youth that I work with who are currently locked up. I wholeheartedly want to see all these young men live in a society that frees them from constant interaction with the criminal legal system and out of the punitive systems of jail and prison. Yet, in a morbid and fucked-up way, the institution is literally saving some of their lives. It is reprehensible, as a society, that our young folks' social safety net is an institution that relies on punishment and removal of freedom to keep them alive. Society has failed these young people, their families, and communities. As I tell everyone, the only reason any of them are in these institutions is because of the zip code where they were born.

Therefore, a large part of abolition—which I know many activists and organizers are doing—is to push for massive investment in anti-poverty legislation, which is where defund intersects with the abolitionist movement. The urgency to reinvest in other aspects of the community, and not solely in policing, punishment, and retribution, is a key part of abolition, which is where reformers and abolitionists can come together.

Abolition democracy is invested in a system that has a limitless social safety net that expands the social welfare state to include resources, tools, and technology to ensure protection and quality of life[198]—instead of the current situation, which is a social safety net comprised of an elephant sitting on wet toilet tissue. Finally, the idea of "safety" is subjective, but it's often not the most vulnerable who are calling for more cops or surveillance, but rather those who already have privilege and advantage in society, who want to subjugate the most marginalized to further penalties. In sum, more police and less social aid will not address the root causes of crime.

JI: I agree: reimagination is crucial. We have become so accustomed to this role of police as a society that we don't often critically question their role. The crucial first step is to get the

reformers and abolitionists in the same room and find common-
ality. I love your idea of "pragmatic abolition" because it might
be an area that abolitionists and reformists find common ground.

Finally, the idea of abolitionist reimagination across the progressive political spectrum is often stifled by absolutes. However, defund moves beyond that and make goals achievable, which
reminds us: "Do not let the perfect become the enemy of the
good."[139]

CHAPTER 6

"Justice Healing / Healing Justice" with Michael and Debbie Davis

Michael and Debbie Davis, who are public speakers, filmmakers, directors, and producers were incarcerated for forty years in the Pennsylvania Department of Corrections system in connection to their membership in MOVE, a radical political organization that is critical of capitalism, supports animal rights, and advocates for environmental justice.[140] They, along with other members and supporters, were targeted by the City of Philadelphia under the direction of police-commissioner-turned-mayor Frank Rizzo, and later by other public officials. Mike and Debbie's four-decade incarceration stemmed from a police attack on the MOVE members' home in West Philadelphia on August 8, 1978, which, according to the evidence, resulted in a police officer being killed by his fellow officers. Ultimately, nine individuals were charged, tried, and convicted of this crime. The political prisoners, known as the MOVE 9, were targeted by a state that saw any form of Black resistance as a threat to White supremacy.

In our conversation, Mike and Debbie discuss their life before MOVE and after their release, including family, love, loss, and what they describe as the concept of "justice healing / healing justice," which emphasizes reconciliation in praxis. Imprisoned

at the height of the twentieth-century Black Power era and released at the peak of the twenty-first-century Black Lives Matter
movement, they provide a keen analysis of and perspective on
the similarities and differences in approaches and strategies for
anti-capitalist and anti-racist activism.

* * *

CJS: *Having served forty years in prison for being part of MOVE,*
you became symbolic figures within leftist and progressive networks
as well as targets of hate and violence by reactionary conservatives.
So there is Mike and Debbie the icons, but also Mike and Debbie the
humans. I've heard you speak about your legacy and not setting out to
be martyrs. Therefore, who were Mike Davis and Debbie Sims before
MOVE, and who are Mike and Debbie Davis today?

DD: Before MOVE, I was a typical teenager who wanted to get
married and have children, go to college, and have a career in
accounting. Unfortunately, my mother couldn't afford to send me
to college. She was raising five children on her own, and it would
be a financial burden, so I declined and got a job. At sixteen, I
met Michael, got serious, and joined MOVE.

MD: I was a knucklehead coming up. I had no plans; didn't think
about a career or save for the future. I had no issues with school
but preferred hanging out. This led me to join the military at
sixteen, but a year later we had both joined MOVE.

We became targets not just because we joined MOVE, but
simply for being minorities. Plenty of folks who are not engaged
in liberation struggles have been victims of the state. For example, Sandra Bland and [George] Floyd were not activists but
still targeted. Anytime someone speaks out against injustice,
they are targeted. Ramsey Orta, who filmed [Eric] Garner being

killed, didn't wake up that day to become an activist.[141] He filmed injustice and was punished for it.

My point is that growing up in our neighborhood made all Black folks targets of police brutality and one moment, instance, or sound bite can change your life forever, as it did for us as well as others like Mumia [Abu-Jamal].[142]

CJS: *While incarcerated, you were deprived of community. When released, what was that initial experience like to be with family, and how has the adjustment to motherhood, fatherhood, and grandparents been?*

DD: It was a corporeal unification; because we had not been united in the physical sense. We have four children, but our son [Michael Africa Jr.] is the most involved right now. Our children were roughly six, five, and two years old when we were locked up. Michael was born in prison. Therefore, because of their ages, they didn't have many memories, but the homecoming was great because we had all our children, family, and supporters to help us. Our reentry was featured in newspapers, and our support system made sure we had everything, so we wanted for nothing. It was a joyous experience that I can't even describe.

MD: I echo Debbie.

I came from a big family with seven siblings. The reality is when we were released, nearly half of my nuclear family had passed on. I contend with a lot of bitterness and regret that there is a forty-year pause in my life. You cannot get back. A person can't come home and assume they will have the same role as when they left. We raised our children on supervised visits and fifteen-minute phone calls, which changes the relationship and incurs gaps. Michael's documentary *40 Years a Prisoner* demonstrates this experience well.

There was a burden placed on our children from the time they were babies—a quest none of them should have had to go through. For example, on every visitation our family had to be searched and treated like prisoners. I wrestle and struggle with that. All our children are amazing, and Michael has a beautiful soul, with such a huge heart, because he has been fighting his entire life to make his family whole. Ultimately, there is still a lot of reconciliation that is needed and a lot we still must reckon with.

CJS: *Why did the burden fall on Michael Jr.?*

DD: Everyone has their own position in a family. Our children all play different roles in our lives advocating for our release, but Mike Jr. just stepped up, if that's the right word, into that more prominent spotlight because of his big heart. Yet, he can't do everything. Our eldest daughters would write letters to the parole board and took me shopping the day I was released to make sure I had the latest fashion trends.

MD: My children are grown with their own families and responsibilities. They were all happy to see us come home, but they have been denied so much. Children, especially little girls, are taught in school and television that Dad is the protector. My daughters were left asking, "Where's Dad?" It's difficult to explain this situation to a child. No matter how many people may have been calling me an activist or brave, my daughters were calling me "missing." I didn't get the opportunity to teach my children how to ride a bicycle, walk them to school, or be there when they needed me most. There is a particular seen and unseen harm that creates a void when you are locked away. To that end, our children are sympathetic to the plight we endured. They understand how we were targeted, and we have had those conversations. Still, conversations can never adequately repair the colossal cavern that a forty-year absence between a parent and child makes.

CJS: *I appreciate you sharing and contextualizing these family dynamics. Beyond this, I've heard you mention that you are "retired activists."*[43] *What does that new role look like?*

DD: I think I said that sort of playing around, but "retired" in the sense that not everybody needs to be on the front lines. Of course, there is always a fight against capitalism but there are many responsibilities in the struggle for liberation. If everyone is on the front lines, then who is caring for the children or other duties. There is no such thing as a "retired activist." Part of our homecoming was to fix our family because it had been broken from a 40-year separation.

MD: When I was a younger man, I was a terrific runner, I could even box a bit too, but I can't run that same distance or punch or defend with the same speed or precision. All this to say, we change our roles, and like sports, we can become coaches, share our experiences, and teach younger generations. We are both over sixty-five [years old], and not everyone can be in the streets. Also, the only time anyone is in the streets is when they see something happen and are outraged. Most activism happens in other sectors of the community. People who are at demonstrations do not see their careers as activists but rather see injustice and feel a sense of urgency to show up at a rally.

CJS: *While imprisoned, were you activists? And were you targeted because of your activism?*

MD: I was very involved.

For example, prisoners were being exploited by the telephone companies. First, all calls are collect calls, meaning you are charged a fee. Second, they add surcharges on top of the preexisting fees. Lastly, all calls made outside of the immediate area surrounding the facility were considered long distance, which added a third fee.

The scheme was that most calls would be dropped [disconnected] within the first minute. Therefore, if you called the person back, a new surcharge would be incurred, and this would repeat several times. In the end, guys were paying possibly fifty dollars or more to use the phone. We began filing grievances and, eventually, a lawsuit, which the Department of Corrections wanted to settle, but we refused. Our complaints finally raised enough attention the company operating this system of exploitation was removed.

I also worked on the issue of the water supply at SCI [State Correctional Institution] –Graterford.[144] The prison was built near a nuclear plant, Limerick Generating Station, that produces smoke clouds that hover over the prison. It is so bad the facility warns staff not to drink the water because of the contamination. Yet, this is the water that the inmates are supposed to drink, bathe in, and wash our clothing in.

The only alternative we had was to buy bottled water, but with restrictions—such as only being allowed a case of water, consisting of twenty bottles, once every three months, for twenty dollars. Therefore, individuals would have to ration the water, which is a human rights violation because you need to drink water daily. Plus, the cost was expensive. For instance, most prison jobs paid seventeen cents an hour for a six-hour workday. Since most individuals cannot afford the water, it adds pressure to family to subsidize the cost of each case of water. Through our activism, we brought attention to the water problems, and eventually the Department of Corrections increased the size of a case from twenty to thirty-five water bottles without increasing the price. A small victory.

Lastly, I graduated from a college program operated through Villanova University and learned carpentry as a trade, as well as other certificates. In terms of being targeted, the MOVE guys were not allowed to do programs when we first arrived. For example, Chuck [Africa] was a terrific boxer, and Pennsylvania had a top-notch prison boxing program. [Former professional boxer] Bernard Hopkins got his start in the Pennsylvania prison box- ing program while he was incarcerated.[145] However, the program traveled the state to different facilities to compete, and since we were considered a "high-level" security risk, we were not allowed to participate. Over time, the guards, staff, and counselors got to know us as individuals and not as these monsters created by the FOP [Fraternal Order of Police] and media.

DD: I was involved with activities such as legal work, gardening, and the dog-training program because it kept me busy, and I liked it.

CJS: *I cannot comprehend the amount of time you spent in prison. You have done more time incarcerated than I have been on the earth.[146] Was there ever a point where you lost hope?*

DD: When we first came home, I thought about how Moses wandered the desert for forty years. So, of course, dying in pris- on was a real thought. I think you would not be human if you didn't think about it, and I can't really believe it when we say it out loud.

I would irrationalize it to myself. I say "*ir*rationalize" because there is nothing rational about the idea of prison. I had to accept the situation, but I never accepted it. But despite how I felt, I still never gave up or gave into those feelings. I kept working.

MD: For many years, I resisted that idea. But at a point, family members get older and begin to pass away. When Merle [Afri- ca] passed, we were at year twenty,[147] and that became a tough reality because it wasn't just [like] people on the outside getting older; we were developing ailments because of the oppressive na- ture of prison. So, sure, I doubted if I might ever make it out, but that never stopped me from writing letters or talking about our experience.

CJS: *How does the trauma you have experienced impact your life moving forward?*

MD: Dealing with trauma is part of our journey, which is connected to longer legacies of collective trauma such as Tulsa and Rosewood [massacres][148] as well as the executions of Michael Brown and George Floyd.

Witnessing state-sanctioned violence makes us collectively cringe and feel all kinds of emotions, which is traumatizing. We try to fill the space that trauma creates the best we can, which means dealing with it daily. However, it is impossible to replace what has been taken from us. The best we can do now is try and ensure others do not have that same experience. As I mentioned earlier, half of my nuclear family transitioned during my four decades imprisoned. Both of my beloved parents, and three siblings. Since being released, two more siblings as well as countless other family members have passed on.

CJS: *In October 2021, you spoke at May Day Space in Bushwick, Brooklyn.[149] During the program, you stated we must collectively strive toward the concept of "justice healing/ healing justice." Can you elaborate on what this phrase means and how we incorporate it into our lives?*

MD: Justice is an action that can only happen when someone acknowledges that they did something wrong; to begin the healing process and rectify a situation.

For example, we have seen attempts, such as the Truth and Reconciliation Commission in South Africa. However, the follow-through did not transpire because those who benefited directly from apartheid and engaged in egregious acts for centuries only had to admit to their role in this segregation system. Yet, outside of that admission, nothing else has been done. They did the first part, but does that matter if admission does not impact their wealth and privilege? I don't see healing occurring.

Justice and healing have a symbiotic relationship, and both must occur for change to occur.

CJS: *In the wake of Black Lives Matter, what was the response to this movement in prison?*

MD: Many were proud. You would see raised fists down the corridor. Guys would be listening to specific cases and, depending on the outcomes, the cell block would erupt in various cheers or boos. There was also this understanding amongst us, collectively, because regardless of which community you come from, everyone on the inside has had negative experiences with police.

CJS: *Responses to MOVE and BLM seem similar regarding reactionary police violence, media criticism, and political threats such as [Mayor] Rizzo and [former President] Trump using terms like "thugs" as placeholders for more explicit racial slurs. Do you see these parallels?*

DD: Definitely. It is history repeating itself. Any system that is unfair or treats one group of life differently is going to [meet] resistance. People are going to fight back.

MD: Violence is America. For instance, Texas public schools do not want to acknowledge that slavery existed.[160] This goes back to the idea of justice healing / healing justice. How can you have reconciliation if you cannot even admit oppression and exploitation occurred? Black Lives Matter came into existence not because injustice suddenly happened, but because the pot has been sitting on the stove simmering. Eventually, it is going to boil over.

It is the same with mass incarceration. It was designed to warehouse generations of folks who are made to work for free as companies profit from that labor. The US prison system has nothing to do with justice or healing. It is no coincidence that poor and minority folks end up in these facilities.

CJS: *I'm reminded of the elaborate system of sending letters to incar-cerated folks in Pennsylvania. The original document is sent to a com-pany, which scans and sends a copy to the person in prison. Therefore, the original is never sent, making the document impersonal because it loses many of the human characteristics of a personalized letter. In the end, the company making the scans is not doing it for free.*[151]

DD: That started in 2018, and I remember thinking this was a new scam. The alleged reason for the change was that a "pow-dery substance" was found in a letter in a men's facility and staff got sick. Whether this really happened or not, I cannot attest, but they developed this new system rather quickly.

It is the same with money orders. In the past, you could send a money order to a prisoner, and it would go into their account. Now, there is this three-way system, which charges a fee based on the percentage of the money being sent to the third party.[152] Usually, you want to cut out the middleman, but they are adding them in. Why else would you make this requirement unless it was profitable for somebody?

MD: In recent years, they allowed technology into the facili-ties only when they figured out how to make a profit, such as closed-circuit email systems.[153] It's a conniving system: if you want to avoid the waiting for a physical letter that is sent to the third-party, you can send a digital message, but every message costs money. The same goes for music. Guys are allowed to have small MP3 players, which can download songs at a premium price—which means asking family and friends for more money. It's not just mass incarceration but mass business.

CJS: *The term "defund" ranges from various reforms to abolitionist stances. Yet this idea, regardless of what it is called, was something the Black Panthers and other revolutionaries of the 1960s and '70s, such as MOVE, advocated for. What do you think changed in the last*

*half century that now has made defund and abolition a more promi-
nent conversation?*

MD: It's the pressure of the people. I would never believe in a system of subjugation that runs roughshod over a community, and that is what the police have been since its inception. I believe in fairness to bring about justice healing. The people need to have a voice in what happens in their communities to heal from traumas inflicted upon them.

When the Panthers came on the scene, they monitored and protected the community, but they also started the breakfast program and education courses.[154] Instead of getting the police or letting someone be taken by the system, the Panthers were attempting to show alternatives to capitalist society. I want to live in a system where folks can take hold of their communities and be responsible for them, not exploited by outside forces. If we can conceptualize a society where love and protection are uplifted, we can begin that healing justice process.

CJS: *Do you see defund as a moment or movement?*

DD: It is like the Olympics. The younger generations have picked up the torch. Time will tell where it goes—whether defund remains the call or something comes to replace it. The important thing to highlight is that it becomes part of a longer legacy, like Harriet Tubman, Martin Luther King, the Panthers, and MOVE. The torch is the movement. Defund might be this generation's moment. But it's all a part of a movement. Honestly, I am still learning about defund and intrigued to see where it goes.

MD: In our day, the media was in cahoots with the political powers, such as the [*Philadelphia*] *Bulletin* and the [*Philadelphia*] *Inquirer* downplaying the devastation Rizzo caused on our family and Black people more generally.

However, today, people can film events and post it on social media, giving an alternative narrative that the mainstream

media cannot lie about. For example, if it wasn't for that brother [Ramsey Orta] filming Eric Garner being choked, the police
would have lied. Even with the video evidence, they still lied.[155]
Each time an incident is filmed and shown over social media, the
movement grows, which is powerful.

CJS: *I agree, the use of recording devices has changed the dynamic
that the reports are no longer a one-sided narrative. For example, the
beating of Delbert [Africa] was captured on camera, showing him as
no threat to law enforcement. Yet they still beat him.[156]*

DD: Yes, the prosecutors tried to charge him with assault on
police. After those images were released, all those charges had
to be thrown out because the film contradicted the police report.

Even still, video evidence alone does not give justice. For
example, the May 13, 1985, bombing of MOVE was recorded.
The city, using a state helicopter, dropped two bombs made of
FBI-supplied materials onto that home, killing eleven people, including five children. Even when it appeared that the courts were
going to hold the city responsible, no city officials or cops were
held accountable. In the end, the state got away with murder.

CJS: *Progressive movements are criticized as not being "nonviolent."
Mainstream politicians evoke Dr. Martin Luther King Jr.'s position
on nonviolence to condemn movements as well as shape a perception
that nonviolence is the only strategy to combat injustice. Yet police are
provided military-grade weapons to inflict violence. How do we combat and address violence against our communities by law enforcement?*

DD: I believe it is the language that needs to change; because
the word "violence" becomes inflammatory, but it takes on different connotations in various situations. America has invaded
countries around the world and called it patriotism, not violence.
During slavery, White folks beat enslaved people; they didn't call
it violence but rather keeping your property in order. Outside
of America, we see what Nazis did to Jewish people and how

the world ignored that violence until it became inconvenient for them. We only see the word "violence" used when a person or group is attempting to defend themselves against abuse or attack.

MD: The state has been the author to dictate and wield violence. Occasionally, someone is made an example, like [George Floyd's killer] Derek Chauvin, to give the illusion of justice within this system. Sending one cop to jail doesn't negate an entire system of violence bestowed on communities. We know it doesn't exist; Debbie and I are living proof of that.

DD: For justice healing to begin, it must start with the self. We must be the change that we want to see in the next person. Our souls are the representation of the person that we want to see in everybody else and what we expect of others. It's that simple. It is about becoming better, learning from mistakes, and growing as a community. We must pass on these types of values to the next generations.

CJS: *During the summer 2020 protests, the City of Philadelphia removed the statue of Frank Rizzo.*[157] *What does the removal of this statue mean to you? Do you think the removal of these sorts of images is the right direction toward liberation?*

MD: It's not just statues but schools, government buildings, and other structures like bridges and tunnels named after oppressors. The symbols that are erected are done with purpose, as a direct challenge to those exploited. It acts as a sort of memorabilia, and they refuse to take down the majority. We hear the excuse of "This is an attack on art," which is nonsense. They want to glorify these individuals as heroes.

In terms of liberation, there must be substantive action behind the removal of these statues. We need to see changes in the law books, legislative bodies, and decisions the courts make. And the community needs to have seats at all those tables. Without that substance, it is the same system—just with less statues.

CJS: *In November 2020, the Philadelphia City Council made a formal apology for the May 1985 bombing of the MOVE home.*[158] *Yet, the city has never apologized to the members of the MOVE 9.*

MD: It goes back to the idea of accountability. We started this conversation about how we served forty years each, which made us accountable for a crime we did not commit. If the city is admitting, or rather apologizing for, wrongdoing, where is the justice in that apology? Philadelphia's apology feels like the Truth and Reconciliation Commission, which is to admit to an injustice without substance.

It took the city nearly forty years to even admit they were wrong. But in that time, look at how many people have been sent to prison. They acknowledge having a corrupt system, but where is the justice? That's what we mean by healing justice. If you are not going to provide some sort of substantive change with the apology, what good is it? Also, to be clear, the city council, who made the apology, are not the individuals responsible for the bombing that murdered children.

Therefore, a public hearing with only an apology—I'm not sure how that is supposed to make me feel. Most of the MOVE 9 are the parents of the children that were in that home. Where is the apology to the parents? The city stole their freedom for forty years and killed their children.

DD: What does that apology mean? It is an offering, and it might be a step forward, but it's hard for me. I helped raised those children. Therefore, the bombing was a personal experience, and an apology isn't going to bring those babies back. The city can take that apology and shove it, because the reality is that situation should never have happened. It should not have taken this long for the city to apologize, and they only did it because of activists and organizations keeping the memory of those events alive. It's not like the city came to this decision on its own but was shamed into acknowledging these murders. Still, no public official, politician, or cop involved in the bombing has been brought to justice. How can a community heal when these acts of violence go unabated?

CJS: *In 2021, it was revealed that remains of some of the children killed in May 1985 had been kept in storage and used by academics and researchers at University of Pennsylvania, the Penn Museum, and Princeton University. This sort of putting the Black body on display is reminiscent of what happened to Sarah Baartman.*[159] *Why do you think these institutions still believe it is appropriate to treat Black remains in this way?*

MD: Black people are viewed as subhuman. Something that is nonhuman can be treated haphazardly. The power structure dismisses compassion and dignity in the name of science. Once again, we see individuals and institutions feign ignorance, and their apologies have no actionable response—which is the opposite of justice healing as Black children's remains were desecrated for decades.

DD: Black folks are treated as specimens. Like how other nonhuman animals are tortured in the name of science as justification. Animals, like humans, have feelings. When a dog barks, it is communicating something. [Even if] we may not understand their language completely, we know what communication looks like. It's the same concept applied to Black people. We have been communicating to White folks for four hundred years the pain we have endured, but like the animals tortured in laboratories, they don't want to listen.

CJS: *Why do you think America has a fixation on continuing mass incarceration, especially keeping elders in prison?*

DD: The system intended for us to die in prison. It was power of the people that kept our case alive, and why we are sitting here today. We weren't released because the system suddenly changed or saw what they did as wrong.

MD: I've found it ironic that it is called "corrections"; because there is nothing corrective about this system. It is a pain and punishment system that thrives on taking away life and humanity.

Debbie and I advocate for the liberation of life, period. We are all connected to each other, animals, and the environment. That is a world we imagined over forty years ago and a world we continue to fight for today by advocating for justice healing / healing justice.

CHAPTER 7

"Defund Saved Us"
with Jasson Perez

Jasson Perez is an abolitionist organizer, researcher, and musical artist. He is a former senior research analyst at the Action Center on Race and the Economy (ACRE)[160] examining the role of mass incarceration and police violence. He is also one-third of the Chicago-based hip hop group BBU. Beyond this, Jasson organizes within various sectors of the community, including the AfroSocialists and Socialists of Color Caucus of the Democratic Socialists of America,[161] and is cofounder of the Black Abolitionist Network.[162]

Our conversation begins with his experiences being justice impacted within the Chicago court and jail systems, his relationship with sobriety, and how he became an organizer. From here, we discuss defund's rise to national recognition, at a pivotal moment in the long-standing struggle for equality fought by working-class people of color, and how defund, as a specific, pragmatic, and strategic organizing goal, became an opportunity to push back against growing opportunism and capitalist profiteering within the Black Lives Matter movement. Next, we talk about the role of "surveillance capitalism" in creating carceral systems that extend beyond traditional brick-and-mortar carceral institutions. Once again, defund, through its repeated demand to shift funds from carceral budgets to social welfare, presents an opportunity to thwart these efforts by corporations and government agencies that want to extend monitoring, and at the same time that we eliminate the need for police and prisons.

Finally, we candidly discuss the role of violence within movement-building and the reality that change does not simply happen organically or through one particular organizing strategy, but rather by making space for arguments that move away from binaries such as "nonviolence" versus "violence." A global vision for a truly socialist, democratized world will come to fruition only through an abolitionist praxis that reimagines justice, replacing harm with care and punishment with protection.

* * *

CJS: *Could you discuss who inspires your politics? Why is music an important form of expression in movement-building?*

JP: I grew up in Chicago. As a child, I was diagnosed with ADHD [attention-deficit/hyperactivity disorder]. In school, I was the class clown and disruptive. At home, I would continually run away to the point that my mom and stepdad turned me over to DCFS [Department of Children and Family Services] and placed me in a group home. There, we did a lot of groups sessions, sports, games, and I began to make music, which gave me purpose when everything else in life didn't make sense. It became my escape.

During this time, I thought a lot of things were my fault, but music helped with my analysis of the world, especially questions like: "Why were all the youth in the group home Latinx and Black?" It was the late '90s, and I was listening to artists like DMX and watching films like *Belly*, which gave me a semblance of understanding that I had a drug problem—something I didn't want to admit to.

When I aged out of the group home at eighteen, I started selling crack. I got caught and ended up doing six months in Cook County Jail and a four-month boot camp program. Since I was a first-time nonviolent offender, I was given an alternative option rather than a seven-year prison sentence. The boot camp was an interesting experience because it was operated by mostly Black men who imposed the "pull yourself up" ideology. It was still part of the carceral apparatus saturated with violence, but something stuck. Once again, like the group home, I only saw Latinx and Black folks in these carceral spaces.

Despite completing the boot camp, I was still a felon and had to serve time on parole. While on parole, I started attending AA [Alcoholics Anonymous] meetings and became interested in underground hip hop. Capital D, a Chicago rapper, resonated because he was talking about recovery and spirituality in his music, which helped me articulate my own feelings, self-worth, and not feel like a lame.

Around this time, I was lucky to get a job with the ACLU [American Civil Liberties Union] and learned about felon discrimination. From there, I became a youth organizer and worked on a campaign to stop police and teachers from being able to go into students' lockers without parents' explicit permission. We lost, but I caught the organizing bug. In sum, organizing and AA saved my life, and I have been sober for over twenty years.

CJS: *As an organizer, you wear many hats. How do your various positions complement and diverge from one another?*

JP: The thing about having ADHD is this feeling of needing to be constantly involved.

A few years ago, I felt burnt out, in a toxic relationship, and put work first. I was not present for my daughter and disenchanted with where the Movement for Black Lives was going, especially with a lack of commitment to traditional organizing. I began seeing too many professional organizers, rather than people

organizing in their workplace or community with an explicit political ideology. It is still a promising movement but just a lot of
work for the "Black left." What I mean is, it is important to not
just be anti-capitalist but explicitly socialist. The reality is that
most people don't wake up every day thinking of themselves as
organizers but rather about their bills and daily tasks. Therefore,
my position as a radical organizer is to figure out how to build
a political project that appeals to a spectrum of working- and
middle-class folks. I look at Bayard Rustin as an inspiration. He
was a member of the National Negro Congress, NAACP [Na-
tional Association for the Advancement of Colored People], and
the Communist Party. Historically within Black progressive collectives, it was common to be part of multiple organizations to
build a united front.

CJS: *When you say "the Black left" and "professional organizers," are
you talking about anyone specifically?*

JP: There are collective leadership failures, and you cannot just
point a finger. Yet, I think the emergence of defund not just as a
spontaneous moment but as a long-term budget campaign is the
best cure toward opportunism. Defund is a strong commitment
to structure-based organizing that is explicit, with clear, meas-
urable goals, that is not just posturing.

Therefore, my critique is that leadership needs to be open to
criticism and not deflect, as well as not just thinking about a
strategy of investment into the organization's coffers. I understand that organizing is not only door-to-door campaigns or
community meetings, but if the majority of your work, or pub-
lic-facing work, is sitting on paid panels or speaking on podcasts,
then that should be a concern for any movement; because not
everything is a right-wing attack.

Abolition is not entertainment. If you are paying individuals
exorbitant amounts of money and the community asks questions, you cannot conveniently claim it is a right-wing smear

campaign. Honestly, the problem is that these critiques began in liberal outlets like *New York Magazine* rather than more leftist publications.[163] And it was easier to claim this story was against the movement rather than taking accountability about personal transactions that reflect poorly on the Movement for Black Lives. Unfortunately, much of the problem is that BLM is operated like a nonprofit managerial company and not like a labor union or old-school [Saul] Alinsky model,[164] with democratically elected officials.

CJS: *The concept of "abolition not as entertainment" is important because abolitionist strategy must consist of self-reflexivity by ensuring that actions and philosophy are in harmony. In terms of abolitionist organizing, how has the global pandemic shifted strategies to sustain movement-building?*

JP: It has been depressing and hard to organize. We take precautions when doing door-knocking canvasing for issues such as student debt, gun-violence prevention, creating a multiracial socialist organization, and a campaign explicitly around saying "defund."

The [COVID-19] pandemic has made it difficult to find organizing spaces to deliberate, strategize, debate, and argue ideas. In the age of "online," it becomes difficult to build networks and organize workers. Therefore, in-person community meetings are essential in developing a political consciousness because it becomes more personal and intimate, versus simply everyone being a tiny box on a computer screen with the temptation to do something else during a meeting and become distracted or disengaged.

CJS: *Speaking of defund as a commitment to organizing, do you see it as a movement or moment?*

JP: Well, the concept of defund has been around for a while. I would never want to take away from that legacy or earlier

iterations, such as divest/invest. However, in this moment, defund came from Kandace Montgomery and the Black Visions
[Collective]'s organizing.[165]

Prior to summer 2020, they had run a defund campaign in
Minneapolis and got money moved into the community. Therefore, in the wake of George Floyd's death, organizers were looking to them for guidance. Originally, Black Visions posted the
"Defund the Police" petition.[166] The murder of Floyd gave defund legitimacy in that moment because it resonated. From there,
the petition was shared thousands if not millions of times, and
defund became part of the movement language and organizing
strategy.

Defund saved us from Black Lives Matter turning into a to-
tally commercialized, amorphous entity. Defund put the politics
back into Black Lives Matter. We cannot forget that BLM began an anti-police, decarceral, abolition organizing movement.
Often, organizing terms can be abstract. Yet defund very much
creates space outside of policing because it confronts budgets
and resources. In other words, we aren't going to accomplish
transformative justice for free; there is a lot of work that goes
into building the communities we want to see. Shifting resources
and reallocating city and municipal budgets can create community accountability models that are not police. Further, defund is
within the power of elected officials, as they can create positions
of full-time public workers that are not police with redistributed
monies.

Defund created conversations. The beauty of defund is that
you could be an abolitionist or not but still support it, as most
people believe addressing police corruption, brutality, and violence is an important step in creating safer communities.

Finally, the best part about defund is that it eviscerates liber-
alism as it cannot be co-opted. Defund is a non-reformist reform
as it would set the stage for more explicit democratizing and
socialist demands.[167] Often, movements, or parts of movements,

become compromised. In this case, defund being co-opted would mean, at minimum, less money for police. Defund as a mainstream tenet entails a paradigm shift that is different than BLM because it is explicitly about reallocation of funding as a concrete measure, above all else. For instance, corporations such as the NBA have gotten behind Black Lives Matter but not defund, because putting "Black Lives Matter" on a T-shirt that can be sold for profit is empty rhetoric and part of larger corporate diversity initiatives that do not actually change the substance of a situation.

CJS: *In November 2021, you tweeted, "I feel kinda exhausted saying this and explaining this, but . . . defund the police / fund our communities is not a radical demand. It's social democratic, at best." Could you expand on this point?*

JP: Defund is the floor.

The tweet was in the context of a response to some *Jacobin* [magazine] folks.[168] I'm tired of arguing for bare minimums because I see how these conversations play out across various communities. In communities of color, concepts like defund are approached in a way of discussing "How are we going to do it?" versus some of these White so-called socialist collectives that ask, "Should we even have things like defund?" The tweet is saying we need to have conversations about these issues and remind folks that defund can be adopted by reformers. Don't get me wrong: defund comes from abolitionist organizing, and we see how mainstream folks back away from defund. For example, all the "progressive" Democrats and "the Squad" [group of US representatives], with the exception of Cori Bush, won't say defund. At the end of the day, we are advocating to take money away from cops, which should not be controversial. It is not like we are targeting a persecuted group of people; it is a group that has done racist, fucked-up shit. In short, the villains are easily identifiable.

Finally, defund goes beyond policing and into all aspects of the carceral apparatus. We should be demanding nonpunitive, restorative accountability policies and not investing in carceral logics, which are imbued into everyday aspects of life. Defund challenges this design to remove the police officers and replace them with mutual aid from the reallocated funding. Again, this is simply the floor.

CJS: *The report* 21st Century Policing,[169] *which you coauthored, discusses the concept of surveillance capitalism. Could you elaborate on how advancements in technology expand the carceral state?*

JP: The report is three pronged, around surveillance, policing, and incarceration as all contribute to the carceral state. We framed the report around surveillance because folks tend to only think about surveillance in the context of terrorism and not in our everyday lives. For example, red-light traffic cameras and household virtual assistant technology—monitoring devices such as Alexa and Ring—are all forms of surveillance.

This technology is extracting money from residents through various fees and fines as well as bringing communities into closer contact with law enforcement with the use of devices like "shot-spotters" [acoustic sensors], facial-recognition software, drones, and other biometric data. Something defund has been clear about is not reallocating funds to these sorts of "e-incarceration" tools.[170] For example, companies like GEO [Group] and Axon are heavily investing in digital surveillance for the purposes of extending carceral systems beyond prison walls, and our goal is to thwart those efforts.

To do this, I subscribe radical flank theory,[171] which is the idea that if you want to get a liberal policy accomplished, you must be at the razor edge of the most radical aspect of an idea. Therefore, whatever the end goals, you must utilize a revolutionary vision without compromise. The problem is that we continually ask for the bare minimum, such as some on the left even questioning if defund is plausible. Of course defund can happen, and we should be demanding it relentlessly if we want to have any sort of liberation, or even substantive reforms.

CJS: *Even prior to defund, some "leftists," not me, have attempted to downplay the role of racism within the criminal legal system and rise of mass incarceration.*[172]

JP: Yeah. I mean, you wrote the best response.[173]

CJS: *Thanks. Where does defund situate itself within these ongoing debates amongst those who claim to be part of "the left" but make reactionary claims?*

JP: My issue is that the goalpost is always moving. At first, it was the issue of BLM as "too identarian." Now the target of criticism has become defund, which focuses on local budgets and re-allocation of municipal spending, moving away from the notion of a race-based movement. Further, defund has the feel of being organized around class, which is what these so-called leftists claim they wanted, and it is still not good enough.

It becomes an issue where there is this notion that White folks, or non-Black folks, have the answers and Black folks should just listen to them. Yet, we know Black folks have a much more intense relationship with police and have a lot of organizing experience in doing anti-police campaigns and strategizing. We should listen to those folks instead of constantly trying to move goalposts to simply criticize movements.

When we organize around defund and talk to Black folks in the community, there are some who want police. It is our job as organizers to figure out how to organize folks around defund that speaks to their experiences through a race, class, and gender analysis, and not simply dismiss them as not "getting it."

CJS: *I've found folks claim to want police, but that is because that is all they know and the only option presented to respond to community harm and violence.*

JP: Exactly. We recognize that not everyone is going to be an abolitionist. Most people agree with having alternatives if presented with options like social workers, traffic aids, and other community workers. The goal is to resolve social issues, which would greatly reduce the role of cops in the community. If we want to take care of violence, we need to expand the public sector, and my hope for defund is to bring about that change.

Defund is combating "crime wave" propaganda, and even though it is not true, statistically, residents want to feel safe. Therefore, organizers, especially larger progressive organizations, must commit to strong messaging, such as unions supporting defund, and criticize copaganda. It's about the sustainability of organizing, not the flash in the pan.

CJS: *While many people do not identify as "abolitionists," a lot of folks espouse abolitionist sentiments. For example, when I did anti-death-penalty organizing, I learned not to ask binary "yes" or "no" questions. Rather, it was better to ask open-ended questions about public safety and use that as a springboard into a deeper discussion of capital punishment to highlight the exorbitant cost, inefficiencies in deterring crime, and callous torture of this practice.*

A second example is when I was doing reentry work in Newark, New Jersey. I brought up abolition, and most did not know what I was talking about until we began discussing the concept and how it related to the work many of the justice-impacted folks wanted to do, like violence interruption, credible messengers, or paralegal certificates to help others.[174] All were engaging in work that moves away from reliance on policing. In sum, movement-building does not happen overnight, and we must vary our approaches; because the first step is going to be conversations.

JP: I came to abolition from my life experiences. I lived in Cabrini-Green [Homes],[175] and we were on welfare. My father was a drug dealer, and we would see all sorts of crime and violence.

Don't get me wrong: violence and responses to crimes are complex. My mother would see sex workers being dragged by their hair and, in that moment, calling the police was the viable option, especially when others did not intervene. That doesn't mean my mom thinks all police are amazing. She has seen the video of cops beating my ass too. Black and Brown folks, especially living in unsafe communities, can see the "both sides" of it. If you need safety and there is only one option, but that option can also be the source of harm, it creates a complicated and tenuous relationship.

Also, police are positioned as community leaders. In Chicago, most block clubs[176] are funded by police because they have grants and resources, which impacts the dynamics of community–police relationships. Not to sound funny, but just because you are a cop does not qualify you as being good in sports or as a mentor/coach. There are many others who could have those jobs in the community. At the end of the day, it's job displacement and copaganda.

My new passion is working with a homie in setting up a leftist AAU [Amateur Athletic Union] basketball team, because we're tired of this cesspool of capitalist, hetero-masculine bullying in the sport. Our vision is to create a transformative-justice commitment to winning and team-building as well as have players engage in reading clubs and other community programs as a holistic approach to athletics, exercise, and mentorship.

CJS: *Socialize the NBA!*

JP: For real. Imagine if we can meld organizing and athletics to create sustainable commitments to communities, rather than liberal capitalism, like having more Black owners or billionaires.

CJS: *What role does violence have as a form of disobedience? In other words, what is the place of violence, or self-defense, as an organizing strategy to create transgressive change?*

JP: I don't like the violence/nonviolence dichotomy. Movements need space to have options. On the one hand, the nonviolent march is a broad spectrum of people that participate at protests. On the other hand, the nonviolence folks need to give space for those who want to engage a different way, especially if the cops begin to use violence. Folks need to be ready to defend themselves, not just retreat.

My politics on abolition is that if you call yourself an abolitionist, then you understand that fighting cops should be within the wheelhouse. The way I was trained up is to think about larger democratized stances, such as de-arrest plans.[177] We want as few people arrested or harmed as possible. In sum: be ready for militant disobedience.

The question we need to ask is how to weave together non-violence/violence instead of this either/or position. My goal as an organizer is to figure out how to do that at a programmatic level, which incorporates elements of nonviolent exercises but makes space for more revolutionary practices. This would mean moving away from this concept that one is pure and the other is not. People are in the streets because fucked-up things happen, and we are passionate, and sometimes passion is not nonviolent. The purpose of strategizing and protest is to create disruption and make things uncomfortable. Therefore, sustained massive disruption in social spaces with enough time and frequency, in a disciplined manner, creates change. While voting is important, we are not going to vote our way out of exploitation. As [political scientist] Frances Fox Piven articulates, disruptive power is the job of organizers.[178]

CJS: *Abolition is a twofold process that begins with the eradication of systems of oppression and their replacement with systems of care.*

Further, abolition creates space for generative discourse to reimagine what public safety looks like outside of traditional punitive guidelines. Therefore, within an abolitionist paradigm, what does a system of care that replaces cops, courts, and prisons look like?

JP: There must be transition phase, which focuses on income, jobs, health care, public education, and democratic control of public institutions and resources. I think of abolition in terms of space: folks need space and safe places to go that do not automatically mean parents lose custody or locking kids in jail. We need to develop spaces where intervention can happen that are not carceral or punitive. To do this, a vision of building out systems of care that are supportive in financial, emotional, and social ways are needed, which would ultimately lead to setting up an abolitionist, socialist, decolonial revolution that topples the United States and regimes that hoard power, resources, and subjugate groups under exploitation and oppression.

CJS: *This is where militancy intersects with your analysis; because that sort of action isn't just going to happen organically.*

JP: For sure. I believe that if people have enough space, time, and income, anything is possible. When we think about the aftermath of the Black freedom movement in the '60s, residents in the United States saw a backlash that included reduced wages, worker power, and benefits. Therefore, a strong militancy can bring us to an abolitionist revolution and social democracy grounded in the democratization of the economy that rids society of groups that would sabotage or harm democracy.

CJS: *As of March 2022, defund is less than two years old. Yet everyone from right-wing pundits to Democrats such as Joe Biden claim defund is dead, which gives hope that this is a sustainable movement.*

JP: Exactly. Why give it that energy?

CJS: *Because they are fucking terrified. During Biden's* [2022] *State of the Union* [address],[179] *he called on this idea of "funding" the police as a direct response to defund. Yet, he did not spend the same energy on other social issues. My optimism is that urgency to downplay defund is because it can happen through the current political process. It is not an abstract thought-exercise but rather budget reallocation, and, as you stated, it is the floor, setting the stage for larger social changes and abolitionist visions.*

Abolitionist Praxis and Visions

The preceding conversations about defund and abolition interrogate a range of nuances and tensions that emerge in collective organizing to eradicate global White supremacist hegemony, eliminate capitalist exploitation, and dismantle systems of state-sanctioned violence in the forms of police and prisons. Defund and abolition have a synergy: defund creates a pathway toward abolition, while abolition gives space for how to imagine defund. Together, this dyad generates powerful opportunities for coalition-building among reformers and abolitionists.

Each interlocutor unpacks different aspects of defund to think deeply about abolition. In chapter 1, Marisol LeBrón articulates how policing, surveillance, and state violence perpetuates harm against marginalized communities to uphold and defend "colonial capitalism." Chapter 2, with Dan Berger, highlights the historical roles various forms of incapacitation have played in creating systems of repression and why abolition is a "both/and" project. In chapter 3, Zellie Imani highlights how twenty-first-century activism has utilized social media to organize, and how to pivot strategies during crisis to continue making safe spaces for residents without police as he advocates his vision that "community is a verb." Chapter 4's interview with Olayemi Olurin delves into what it means to be an abolitionist working within the criminal

justice system, and how to use this position as a public defender to assist defendants and subvert the system at every turn: as
she articulates, "Those who can, must!" In chapter 5, Jonathan
Ilan highlights how creativity, particularly in the form of music, is important to movement-building and creating sustainable
coalition among reformers and abolitionists alike, which brings
about "pragmatic abolition." Chapter 6, with Michael and Debbie
Davis, offers introspection into what it means to endure decades
as political prisoners and the corresponding impacts on the self,
family, and broader community. Connecting the conditions of
their incarceration to the challenges of present-day racial justice movements, the Davises draw upon their lived experience to
outline their vision for what they call "justice healing / healing
justice." Finally, chapter 7, with Jasson Perez, examines the potential of labor organizing to combat opportunism within movements, along with the role of defund in thwarting co-optation
and pushing back against "surveillance capitalism." In all these
conservations, each person added value to the larger discussion
of defund and its connection to abolition.

In each interview, the through line is clear: together, we can
build a better world. Indeed, each chapter highlights that we
have the tools, resources, and theory to provide for all beings,
care for the planet, and envision spaces that prioritize care over
harm. While change may take time, motivated and inspired
struggle moves us collectively toward abolitionist futures and
defund becomes an important catalyst for this process. Ultimately, abolition does not stop at dismantling the current system;
rather, it *begins* by creating a world that reduces stratification
and violence, constructing new systems that are not predicated
on retribution, exploitation, and profit but rather motivated by
reconciliation, care, and mutual aid. Complementarily, defund
provides the blueprint for shifting resources, budgets, and tools
into abolitionist spaces.

Finally, since summer 2020, we have seen a cascade of abolitionist praxis and visions as well as reminded of how previous generations envisioned abolitionist futures. Scholar and organizer Dylan Rodríguez articulates the historical evolution of abolitionist praxis writing, "The long historical praxis of abolition is grounded in a Black radical genealogy of revolt and transformative insurgency against racial chattel enslavement and the transatlantic trafficking of captive Africans."[180] Praxis has found its way into mainstream entertainment, if implicitly, as seen in the ABC television sitcom series *Abbott Elementary*. Set in an under-funded, majority-Black and -Latinx Philadelphia elementary school, the show's first season does not include the appearance or recognition of police as a response to dispute or conflict. As recounted in the introduction, a student in my class asked, "Can you describe any situation where there are no police?" Quinta Brunson, the show's creator, has done just this: envisioned a world without police.

Coming back to Rodríguez's discussion of praxis, abolition is not solely political but artistic. He offers the observation that abolition is "an art form, the kind of creative truth that mixes the stuff of history into memory, survival, breath, and stubborn, vexed, and often-nourishing community that constantly escapes the guarantees of any organizing plan."[181] In sum, abolition not only embraces the imaginative; it *is* imagination.

The radical imagination has consistently envisioned a world without police. Consider, for example, African American artist Romare Bearden, famous for using paint and collage, his works speak to the Black experience in America.

Notably, Bearden's drawing *The Block*, created in 1971, articulates an abolitionist praxis, providing a powerful allegory that connects past, present, and future. On six individual panels, Bearden highlights both the sacred and mundane aspects of life in and around the Harlem community with imagery of a barbershop, apartment buildings, and day-to-day life such as a

mother putting her child to sleep, a woman bathing, and children playing. What is noticeably absent in this imaginary is the
presence of police or state-sanctioned surveillance. Bearden, using, "cut and pasted printed, colored, and metallic papers, pho-
tostats, graphite, ink marker, gouache, watercolor, and ink on
Masonite,"[182] creates a world without police in the Harlem community that has historically been a target of police surveillance
as well as a location of concentrated incarceration.[183] Whether
intentional or not, the omission of police in this landscape of the
"block" is profound. The "block" within urban landscapes is the
place information is passed, shared, and retained. It is the space
and place in which life lessons are learned, character is built, and
traditions performed.

As the celebrated urban grassroots activist Jane Jacobs ob-
served, the block is essential to life.[184] Further, novelist and play-
wright, James Baldwin, a Harlem native, and longtime friend
of Bearden, having met while both were living in Paris in 1950,
spoke to the beauty of Bearden's work. In 1978, the two men sat in
conversation with Alvin Ailey and Albert Murray recalling their
experiences and relationships to artforms. Here, Baldwin stated,
"[T]o reach back and claim what has always been yours; yet with
that same gesture, you're empowered to move forward…It was
an extraordinary thing to me in 1950 until this hour, from the
first things I saw of yours until the last show I saw of yours." [185]
Baldwin recognized the brilliance and importance of Bearden's
art in shaping how we affirm the past, make sense of the present,
and assert our future. In sum, Bearden's rejection of an occu-
pied force that creates disruption and disharmony emblematizes
defund's goal of removing police from communities as well as
abolitionist visions that reimagine a world without police.

Ultimately, I hope this book serves in three ways: first, to
illustrate that defund is a powerful first step toward abolition
as it advocates shifting money from police, courts, and corrections into nonpunitive sectors of society; second, to reaffirm, as

Mariame Kaba observes, that hope is a discipline, essential to the sustainment of our collective movement(s)[186] and finally, to serve as a reminder that we all cannot do everything, but we can all do *something*. In the end, together, we will win.

Acknowledgments

I'm humbled and grateful to be writing my second acknowledgments page in less than a year. This was a year of writing, which comes with all the joy, excitement, and pleasure of completing a manuscript. Conversely, this also means sleepless nights, stress, frustration, and doubt: writing is a roller coaster with various peaks and valleys. I'm thankful to my community, friends, and family, who continue to support my work. There are never enough words to show this appreciation, and I am thankful to all those who have touched my life, whether listed or not.

First, I would like to thank Haymarket Books for taking this chance with me, as this book came about in somewhat nontraditional manner. I am appreciative of Anthony Arnove, Sean Larson, Katy O'Donnell, Jameka Williams, and Sam Smith, who have believed in my vision and given me the breadth and range to create this work.

Second, I am indebted to all the voices that contributed to this work. In most cases, it was a shot in the dark when I reached out to each person hoping they would agree to be part of this book. Your voices, analyses, and critical understanding of social movements, carceral logics, and defund makes this book work. Thank you, Dan Berger, Debbie Davis, Mike Davis, Jonathan Ilan, Zellie Imani, Marisol LeBrón, Olayemi Olurin, and Jasson Perez.

Next, I am thankful to Hunter College–CUNY, PSC–CUNY, Research Foundation CUNY, and my colleagues in the sociology department for support in the process of writing this manuscript. More specifically, I appreciate my colleagues and peers who read early drafts or engaged in discussions about this manuscript including Marc Lamont Hill, Tamara K. Nopper, Alexandrea J. Ravenelle, and Alex Vitale. Additionally, I'd like to thank Emily LeGrand, who provided the index for this book.

Friends are important to writing, not only as individuals with whom you can complain and procrastinate, but also as a source of encouragement. Thank you, Sean Allen, Greg Anderson, Kester Barrow, Gigi Blanchard, Karl Brisseaux, Mario Campo, Zahir Carrington, Madison Cline, Jonathan Edwards, Michael Fernandez, Tennyson Hinds, Isaiah Jennings, Curtiss Jones, Jeff London, Gabriel Lugo, Xavier Lugo, Anna Orchard, Cameron Rasmussen, Eric Reeves, Garret E. Richardson, Marcelino Rodriguez, Shaun Redwood, Ahmed Salim, Terrence Talley, Kahron Walker, Grace Woods, and Nikki Woods.

Finally, I must thank my family, the Pietruszkas, the Stampors, my aunt Karen Nagel-Hedtmann, uncle Udo Hedtmann; my late grandmother, Mary Nagel, and her late partner, my surrogate grandfather, Michael Thomas; my mother and father, Cheryl Nagel-Smiley and Calvin Smiley Jr.; my wife, Maria Pietruszka-Smiley; and our fur babies: our late beagle, Molly (2009–2022), our cats, Stella and Rajah, and the newest addition to our family, our mixed-breed rescue pup, Wesley.

Notes

INTRODUCTION

1   In May 2020, George Floyd was killed by police officers in Minneapolis, Minnesota, after being accused of attempting to pass a counterfeit twenty-dollar bill at a convenience store. In March 2020, Breonna Taylor was killed in Lexington, Kentucky, after police entered the wrong apartment and shot her while she laid in bed. In February 2020, Ahmaud Arbery was chased by three White men while he was jogging and gunned down. For more on all these cases, see Marc Lamont Hill, *We Still Here: Pandemic, Policing, Protest, and Possibility* (Chicago: Haymarket, 2020); Angela Y. Davis et al., *Abolition. Feminism. Now.* (Chicago: Haymarket, 2022); Robert Samuels and Toluse Olorunnipa, *His Name Is George Floyd: One Man's Life and the Struggle for Racial Justice* (New York: Viking, 2022); Kimberlé Crenshaw and African American Policy Forum, *#SayHerName: Black Women's Stories of State Violence and Public Silence* (Chicago: Haymarket, 2023).

2   "Yes 4 Minneapolis," Black Visions, https://www.blackvisionsmn.org/ yes4mn.

3   Martin Kaste, "Minneapolis Voters Reject a Measure to Replace the City's Police Department," *NPR*, November 3, 2021, https://www.npr. org/2021/11/02/1051617581/minneapolis-police-vote.

4   Matt Furber, John Eligon, and Audra D. S. Burch, "Minneapolis Police, Long Accused of Racism, Face Wrath of Wounded City," *New York Times*, May 27, 2020, https://www.nytimes.com/2020/05/27/us/ minneapolis-police.html.

5   Furber, Eligon, and Burch, "Minneapolis Police."

6   US Department of Justice, *Federal Reports on Police Killings: Ferguson, Cleveland, Baltimore, and Chicago* (New York: Melville House, 2017).

7   Keeanga-Yahamtta Taylor, *From #BlackLivesMatter to Black Liberation* (Chicago: Haymarket, 2019), 127.

8   United States Department of Justice Civil Rights Division and United States Attorney's Office District of Minnesota Civil Division, *Investigation of the City Of Minneapolis and the Minneapolis Police Department* (Washington D.C., 2023), 1. The report highlights 1. The use of excessive force, 2. Unlawful discrimination against Black and Native American people, 3. Violation of rights of people engaged in

protected speech, and 4. Discrimination against people with behavioral
health disabilities when responding to calls for assistance.

9   See CUNY For Abolition and Safety's Link Tree: https://linktr.ee/
      cunyforabolition.

10   Angela Y. Davis, *Are Prisons Obsolete?* (New York: Seven Stories, 2003);
      Angela Y. Davis, *Abolition Democracy: Beyond Empires, Prisons, and
      Torture* (New York: Seven Stories, 2005).

11   Mariame Kaba, *We Do This 'Til We Free Us: Abolitionist Organizing and
      Transforming Justice* (Chicago: Haymarket, 2021).

12   Kaba, *We Do This 'Til We Free Us*, 26.

13   Kaba, *We Do This 'Til We Free Us*, 27.

14   Kaba, *We Do This 'Til We Free Us*, 27.

15   I credit Dan Berger for this creative spelling of "movement" and
      "moment" via email correspondence on January 18, 2022.

16   See Jeff Goodwin and James M. Jasper, eds., *The Social Movements
      Reader: Cases and Concepts* (Hoboken, NJ: Wiley-Blackwell, 2009).

17   See Devah Pager, *Marked: Race, Crime, and Finding Work in the Era
      of Mass Incarceration* (Chicago: University of Chicago Press, 2007);
      Michelle Alexander, *The New Jim Crow: Mass Incarceration in the
      Age of Colorblindness* (New York: The New Press, 2010); Keeanga-
      Yamahtta Taylor, *Race for Profit: How Banks and the Real Estate Industry
      Undermined Black Homeownership* (Chapel Hill: University of North
      Carolina Press, 2021).

18   There is ongoing debate about the relevancy of #defund outside of the
      US paradigm. See Megan McElhone et al., "Defund—not Defend—the
      Police: A Response to Fleetwood and Lea," *Howard Journal of Crime
      and Justice* (2023), https://doi.org/10.1111/hojo.12508.

19   Joseph R. Biden, "State of the Union," The White House, March 1, 2022,
      https://www.whitehouse.gov/state-of-the-union-2022.

20   Alexi McCammond, "Rep. Cori Bush Isn't Backing Down on 'Defund
      the Police' Slogan," *Axios*, February 8, 2022, https://www.axios.
      com/2022/02/09/cori-bush-defund-police-2022-midterms.

21   "Back the blue" is a conservative phrase used to show support for law
      enforcement.

22   Eric Garcia and John Bowden, "Majorie Taylor Greene Tweets Upside
      Down American Flag amid GOP Fury at Raid on Trump's Mar-a-
      Lago Home," *Independent*, August 9, 2022, https://www.independent.
      co.uk/news/world/americas/us-politics/marjorie-greene-trump-fbi-
      mar-b2141116.html.

23   Sahil Kapur, "Donald Trump Calls for Defunding Federal Police after
      His Arrest in New York," *NBC News*, April 5, 2023, https://www.
      nbcnews.com/politics/congress/donald-trump-calls-defunding-federal-
      police-arrest-new-york-rcna78301.

24   Alex Vitale, *The End of Policing*, rev ed. (London: Verso, 2021).

25   Laurena Bernabo, "Copaganda and Post-Floyd TVPD: Broadcast

Television's Response to Policing in 2020," *Journal of Communication* 72, no. 4 (August 2020): 488–96, https://doi.org/10.1093/joc/jqac019.

26   Ida B. Wells, "Lynch Law in All Its Phases" (February 13, 1893), *Voices of Democracy: The U.S. Oratory Project*, July 30, 2007, https://voicesofdemocracy.umd.edu/wells-lynch-law-speech-text/.

27   See Bridget R. Cooks and Sarah Watson, *The Black Index* (Munich: Hirmer Publishers, 2021).

28   Crenshaw and African American Policy Forum, *#SayHerName*.

29   Jen Kirby, "'Black Lives Matter' Has Become a Global Rallying Cry against Racism and Police Brutality," *Vox*, https://www.vox.com/2020/6/12/21285244/black-lives-matter-global-protests-george-floyd-uk-belgium.

30   Haroon Siddique and Clea Skopeliti, "BLM Protesters Topple Statue of Bristol Slave Trader Edward Colson," *Guardian*, June 7, 2020, https://www.theguardian.com/uk-news/2020/jun/07/blm-protesters-topple-statue-of-bristol-slave-trader-edward-colston.

31   Kirby, " 'Black Lives Matter.' "

32   Danica Coto, "Puerto Rico Questions Spain's legacy as Statues Tumble in US," *AP News*, July 11, 2020, https://apnews.com/article/europe-latin-america-ap-top-news-travel-caribbean-21139ea13a1957ce4ea6d0db5679b786.

33   Larry Celona and David Meyer, "'F—k Columbus' Graffiti Found on Manhattan Statue after Cop Barricades Removed," *New York Post*, https://nypost.com/2021/04/18/f-k-columbus-graffiti-found-on-nyc-statue-after-barricades-removed.

34   Erin L. Thompson, *Smashing Statues: The Rise and Fall of America's Public Monuments* (New York: W. W. Norton, 2022).

35   Hill, *We Still Here.*

36   Wilson Wong, "More than 2,000 New Jersey Inmates Released to Slow Spread of Coronavirus in Prisons," *NBC News*, November 4, 2020, https://www.nbcnews.com/news/us-news/more-2-000-new-jerscy-inmates-released-slow-spread-coronavirus-n1246388.

37   Naomi Klein, *The Shock Doctrine: The Rise of Disaster Capitalism* (London: Picador 2007); Aimee Picchi, "10 Richest Billionaires Doubled Their Wealth during Pandemic, Oxfam says," *CBS News*, January 16, 2022, https://www.cbsnews.com/news/billionaires-double-wealth-covid-pandemic.

38   See Hill, *We Still Here*; Kaba, *We Do This 'Til We Free Us*; Vitale, *End of Policing*; Derecka Purnell, *Becoming Abolitionists: Police Protests and The Pursuit of Freedom* (New York: Astra House, 2021); Colin Kaepernick, *Abolition for the People: The Movement for a Future without Policing and Prisons* (New York: Kaepernick Publishing, 2021); Davis et al., *Abolition. Feminism. Now*; Ruth Wilson Gilmore, *Abolition Geography: Essays towards Liberation* (London: Verso, 2022); Mariame Kaba and Andrea J. Ritchie, *No More Police: A Case for Abolition* (Chicago: Haymarket, 2022); Ray Acheson, *Abolishing State Violence: A World beyond Bonds,*

Borders, and Cages (Chicago: Haymarket, 2022); and Kelly Hayes and Mariame Kaba, *Let This Radicalize You: Organizing and the Revolution of Reciprocal Care* (Chicago: Haymarket, 2023).

39 Olúfémi O. Táíwò, *Elite Capture: How the Powerful Took Over Identity Politics* (Chicago: Haymarket, 2022), 4–5.

40 Kari Paul, "Amazon Says 'Black Lives Matter.' But the Company Has Deep Ties to Policing," *Guardian*, June 9, 2020, https://www. theguardian.com/technology/2020/jun/09/amazon-black-lives-matter-police-ring-jeff-bezos.

41 Naomi Murkawa, Say Their Names, Support Their Killers: Police Reform After the 2020 Black Lives Matter Uprisings," *UCLA Law Review* 69 (September 2023): 1430-1485.

42 Mark Engler and Paul Angler, "André Gorz's Non-Reformist Reforms Show How We Can Transform the World Today," *Jacobin*, July 22, 2021, https://jacobin.com/2021/07/andre-gorz-non-reformist-reforms-revolution-political-theory. See also: Ruth Wilson Gilmore, *Golden Gulag: Prisons, Surplus, Crisis, and Opposition in Globalizing California* (Berkeley: University of California Press, 2007).

43 See Hill, *We Still Here*; Angel Davis, *Freedom Is a Constant Struggle: Ferguson, Palestine, and the Foundations of a Movement* (Chicago: Haymarket, 2016); Kaba, *We Do This 'Til We Free Us*.

CHAPTER 1

44 See Marisol LeBrón, *Policing Life and Death: Race, Violence, and Resistance in Puerto Rico* (Berkeley: University of California, 2019); Marisol LeBrón, *Against Muerto Rico: Lessons from Verano Boricua* (Toa Baja, PR: Editora Educación, 2021); Yarimar Bonilla and Marisol LeBrón, *Aftershocks of Disaster: Puerto Rico before and after the Storm* (Chicago: Haymarket, 2019).

45 See LeBrón, *Policing Life and Death*.

46 Zaire Z. Dinzey-Flores, *Locked In, Locked Out: Gated Communities in a Puerto Rican City* (Philadelphia: University of Pennsylvania Press, 2013).

47 See Rosario Farajado, "A Closer Look at the UPR's FY2022 Budget: Two Different Vies from the FOMB and UPR President," *Weekly Journal*, June 9, 2021, https://www.theweeklyjournal.com/online_ features/a-closer-look-at-the-upr-s-fy2022-budget/article_0f6c0e66-c88c-11eb-968a-07e02d058bf7.html.

48 See Patricia Mazzei and Frances Robles, "Ricardo Rosselló, Puerto Rico's Governor, Resigns after Protests," *New York Times*, July 24, 2019, https://www.nytimes.com/2019/07/24/us/rossello-puerto-rico-governor-resigns.html.

49 Acuerdo de Paz in Loíza is an evidence-based project that seeks to minimize violence in the city of Loíza. This project is part of Taller Salud, which is a community-based feminist organization dedicated to improving women's access to health care, to reducing violence within

the community and to encourage economic growth through education and activism. See: https://www.tallersalud.com/?lang=en.

50 Cheryl LaBash, "Free Puerto Rico! Drop Charges on Elimar Chardón Sierra," *Struggle for Socialism*, March 15, 2019, https://www.struggle-la-lucha.org/2019/03/05/free-puerto-rico-drop-charges-on-elimar-chardon-sierra/.

51 Coto, "Puerto Rico Questions Spain's Legacy."

52 See Colectivo Ilé an anti-racist and decolonial organization with the purpose of educating to eradicate racism and all its manifestations through community organizing and workshops: http://colectivo-ile.org/.

53 Amanda Alcántara, "'Twenty Years Later, Tego Calderón's 'El Abayarde' Still Embodies the Powerful, Raw Spirit of Reggaeton, *Rolling Stone*, November 1, 2022, https://www.rollingstone.com/music/music-latin/tego-calderon-el-abayarde-20th-anniversary-1234622295/

54 See Rebecca Speare-Cole, "American Tourist Killed in La Perla, Puerto Rico, Named as Tariq Quadir Loat," *Newsweek*, April 28, 2021, https://www.newsweek.com/la-perla-puerto-rico-tourist-killed-american-tariq-quadir-loat-1587038.

55 See Meghan G. McDowell and Luis A. Fernandez, " 'Disband, Disempower, and Disarm': Amplifying the Theory and Practice of Police Abolition," *Critical Criminology* 26, no. 3 (2018): 373–91, https://doi.org/10.1007/s10612-018-9400-4.

56 See #8CantWait: https://8cantwait.org/.

57 See Marta Caminero-Santangelo, "Latinidad," in *The Routledge Companion to Latino/a Literature*, ed. Suzanne Bost and Frances R. Aparicio (New York: Routledge, 2013), 13–24.

58 See Associated Press, "Arizona Border Activist Who Gave Water to Migrants Faces Second Trial," *Guardian*, November 12, 2019, https://www.theguardian.com/us-news/2019/nov/12/arizona-migrants-trial-scott-warren.

CHAPTER 2

59 See Dan Berger, *Stayed on Freedom: The Long History of Black Power through One Family's Journey* (New York: Basic Books, 2023); Dan Berger and Toussaint Losier, *Rethinking the American Prison Movement* (New York: Routledge, 2017); Dan Berger, *Captive Nation: Black Prison Organizing in the Civil Rights Era* (Chapel Hill: University of North Carolina Press, 2016); Dan Berger, *The Struggle Within: Prisons, Political Prisoners, and Mass Movements in the United States* (Binghamton, NY: PM Press, 2014); Dan Berger and Emily Hobson, eds., *Remaking Radicalism: A Grassroots Documentary Reader of the United States, 1973—2001* (Athens: University of Georgia Press, 2020).

60 For more on George Jackson, see George Jackson, *Blood In My Eye*

(Baltimore: Black Classic, 1996); George Jackson, *Soledad Brother: The Prison Letters of George Jackson* (Chicago: Lawrence Hill, 1994).

61   See the Free Alabama Movement: https://freealabamamovement. wordpress.com/.

62   See Ruth Wilson Gilmore, *Golden Gulag: Prisons, Surplus, Crisis, and Opposition in Globalizing California* (Berkeley: University of California Press, 2007).

63   See David Graeber, *Bullshit Jobs: A Theory* (New York: Simon & Schuster, 2019).

64   See Douglas A. Blackmon, *Slavery by Another Name: The Re-enslavement of Black Americans from the Civil War to World War II* (New York: Anchor, 2009); Karen Shapiro, *A New South Rebellion: The Battle against Convict Labor in the Tennessee Coalfields, 1871—1896* (Chapel Hill: University of North Carolina Press, 1998).

65   Rikers Island is the site of New York City's largest jail.

66   See Free Alabama Movement, "Let the Crops Rot in the Fields (February 17, 2018), available at https://libcom.org/article/let-crops-rot-fields; Dan Berger, "Rattling the Cages," *Jacobin*, November 18, 2016, https://jacobin.com/2016/11/prison-strike-slavery-attica-racism-incarceration.

67   See Paige St. John, "Four Inmates on Hunger Strike Require Medical Attention," *Los Angeles Times*, July 18, 2013, https://www.latimes.com/politics/la-xpm-2013-jul-18-la-me-ff-4-hunger-strike-inmates-require-medical-attention-20130718-story.html; Perilous, "2016 National Prison Strike: Uprising at Kinross Correctional Facility, Michigan," *Perilous Chronicle*, September 10, 2016, https://perilouschronicle. com/2016/09/10/uprising-at-kinross-correctional-facility-michigan/.

68   Our conversation took place on January 13, 2022. As of this conversation, criminal trials of participants in the insurrection which took place on January 6, 2021 are ongoing. Several insurrectionists have received lengthy sentences. See Sareen Habeshian, "Here are the harshest punishments yet for Jan. 6 rioters," *Axios*, September 5, 2023, https://www.axios.com/2023/09/01/jan-6-longest-sentences-list.

69   See Amrit Cheng, "Crystal Mason Thought She Had the Right to Vote. Texas Sentenced Her to Five Years in Prison for Trying," *ACLU*, n.d., https://www.aclu.org/issues/voting-rights/fighting-voter-suppression/crystal-mason-thought-she-had-right-vote-texas.

70   See Natasha Lennard, "Right-Wing Judges Say It's 'Harmless' to Label Climate Activist a Terrorist," *Intercept*, June 8, 2022, https://theintercept.com/2022/06/08/dakota-pipeline-protester-jessica-reznicek-terrorism.

71   See Luc Cohen, "NY Lawyers Plead Guilty in Molotov Cocktail Case; Shorter Sentences Likely," June 2, 2022, *Reuters*, https://www.reuters. com/legal/government/ny-lawyers-plead-guilty-molotov-cocktail-case-shorter-sentences-likely-2022-06-02/.

72   This interview took place in January 2022. Sundiata Acoli was released in May 2022.

73   For more on these organizing and advocacy efforts in New York, see the Release Aging People in Prison campaign: https://rappcampaign.com.

74   See Autodidcact 17, "Former Political-P.O.W. Robert Seth Hayes Passes," *Amsterdam News*, January 2, 2020, https://amsterdamnews.com/news/2020/01/02/former-political-pow-robert-seth-hayes-passes/.

75   See David Johnston, "F.B.I. Agents Rally against Possible Clemency," *New York Times*, December 16, 2000, https://www.nytimes.com/2000/12/16/us/fbi-agents-rally-against-possible-clemency.html.

76   Dan Berger, "SNCC's Unruly Internationalism," *Boston Review*, November 16, 2021, https://www.bostonreview.net/articles/snccs-unruly-internationalism.

77   See Zeynep Tufekci, *Twitter and Tear Gas: The Power and Fragility of Networked Protest* (New Haven: CT, Yale University Press, 2017).

78   Dan Berger, "Beyond Innocence: US Political Prisoners and the Fight Against Mass Incarceration," *TruthOut*, July 24, 2015, https://truthout.org/articles/beyond-innocence-america-s-political-prisoners-and-the-fight-against-mass-incarceration/.

79   See Richard Fausset, "Two in Arbery Case Sentenced Again to Life in Prison; Third Man Gets 35 Years," *New York Times*, August 8, 2022, https://www.nytimes.com/2022/08/08/us/arbery-killer-sentencing.html

80   Danielle Sered, *Until We Reckon: Violence, Mass Incarceration, and a Road to Repair* (New York: The New Press, 2021).

81   Daniel Denvir, interview with Jane McAlevey, *The Dig* (podcast), March 27, 2019, https://thedigradio.com/podcast/strike-with-jane-mcalevey.

CHAPTER 3

82   See Black Lives Matter–Paterson: https://blacklivesmatterpaterson.org.

83   For more information on the work being done by Black Lives Matter–Paterson and local community organizers see: Ricardo Kaulessar, "Black Lives Matter chapter in NJ launching youth-led summer camp for future activists," *northjersey.com*, June 3, 2021, https://www.northjersey.com/story/news/local/2021/06/03/black-lives-matter-paterson-nj-youth-summer-camp-future-activists/7447311002/; Rebecca King, "Community fridge founded by Black Lives Matter Paterson helps feed homeless people," *northjersey.com*, January 27, 2022, https://www.northjersey.com/story/news/passaic/paterson/2022/01/27/black-lives-matter-paterson-nj-community-fridge-homeless-people/6570911001/; Steve Lenox, "Paterson Healing Collective Sets out to 'Stop the Bleed' and the Violence," *TapintoPaterson*, March 28, 2021, https://www.tapinto.net/towns/paterson/sections/law-and-justice/articles/paterson-healing-collective-sets-out-to-stop-the-bleed-and-the-violence;

Darren Tobia, "Paterson BLM opens harm reduction center to stem tide of drug overdoses, HIV infection," *northjersey.com*, April 17, 2023, https://www.northjersey.com/story/news/paterson-press/2023/04/17/paterson-blm-opens-drug-harm-reduction-center-for-safe-needle-exchange/70118740007/.

84   See Dean Spade, *Mutual Aid: Building Solidarity during This Crisis (and the Next)* (London: Verso, 2020).

85   See Oxfam International, "Ten richest men double their fortunes in pandemic while incomes of 99 percent of humanity fall," *oxfam.org*, January 17, 2022, https://www.oxfam.org/en/press-releases/ten-richest-men-double-their-fortunes-pandemic-while-incomes-99-percent-humanity#:~:text=Billionaires'%20wealth%20has%20risen%20more,billionaire%20wealth%20since%20records%20began.

86   A reference to the abolition of slavery in the United States.

87   See City of Paterson, *New Jersey CY2022 Budget as Introduced*, 2022, https://www.patersonnj.gov/egov/apps/services/index.egov?view=detail;id=42.

88   See Kimberlé Williams Crenshaw et al., "Say Her Name: Resisting Police Brutality against Black Women," Columbia Law School Faculty Paper, 2015, https://scholarship.law.columbia.edu/cgi/viewcontent.cgi?article=4235&context=faculty_scholarship.

89   See Reis Thebault, "A Cop Slapped a Suicidal Hospital Patient. Then the Video Emerged," *Washington Post*, April 4, 2019, https://www.washingtonpost.com/nation/2019/04/05/cop-slapped-suicidal-hospital-patient-then-video-emerged/; Eric Levenson, "Jameek Lowery Was Paranoid and Pleaded with Police for Help. He Died Two Days Later," *CNN*, January 10, 2019, https://www.cnn.com/2019/01/09/us/paterson-new-jersey-death-police-protest/index.html.

90   See "Qualified Immunity," Equal Justice Initiative, https://eji.org/issues/qualified-immunity/.

91   As of March 17, 2022.

92   See Elizabeth Alexander, *The Trayvon Generation* (New York: Grand Central Publishing, 2022).

93   See Marcia Mundt, Karen Ross, and Charla M. Burnett, "Scaling Social Movements through Social Media: The Case of Black Lives Matter," *Social Media and Society* 4, no. 4 (October–December 2018): 1–14, https://doi.org/10.1177/2056305118807911.

CHAPTER 4

94   The Legal Aid Society is the oldest and largest provider of legal aid in the United States, based in New York City. For more information: https://legalaidnyc.org/

95   Olayemi Olurin, "Law and Order Taught Americans to Root for the Police," *Teen Vogue*, December 8, 2021, https://www.teenvogue.com/story/law-and-order-policing-media.

96 See Jeff Shantz, "Insurgent Criminology in a Period of Open Social War," *Radical Criminology* 6 (2016): 1–10.

97 See New York City Department of Corrections population demographics reports: https://www.nyc.gov/site/doc/about/demographics-reports.page.

98 The operating budget for New York City Department of Corrections Fiscal Year 2022 is $1.2 billion. See New York State Comptroller, "Issues Facing New York City's Agencies: New York City Department of Corrections," n.d., https://www.osc.state.ny.us/files/reports/osdc/pdf/doc-issue-brief.pdf.

99 A remake and revision of the sitcom *The Fresh Prince of Bel-Air* (NBC, 1990–96).

100 See Mariame Kaba, *We Do This 'Til We Free Us: Abolitionist Organizing and Transforming Justice* (Chicago: Haymarket, 2021); Mariame Kaba and Andrea J. Ritchie, *No More Police: A Case for Abolition* (Chicago: Haymarket, 2022).

101 Angela Y. Davis, *Are Prisons Obsolete?* (New York: Seven Stories, 2003).

102 See Prison Policy Initiative, "Prisons of Poverty: Uncovering the Pre-incarceration Incomes of the Imprisoned," July 9, 2015, https://www.prisonpolicy.org/reports/income.html.

103 See Associated Press, "Bahamas to Increase Minimum Wage, Implement Price Controls," *ABC News*, October 12, 2022, https://abcnews.go.com/International/wireStory/bahamas-increase-minimum-wage-implement-price-controls-91381687#:~:text=The%20minimum%20wage%20will%20increase,Philip%20Davis%20announced%20Tuesday%20night.

104 See Close Rikers: https://www.campaigntocloserikers.org.

105 See "A Roadmap to Closing Rikers," City of New York, https://rikers.cityofnewyork.us.

106 See Vera Institute of Justice, *A Look Inside the New York City Correction Budget*, 2021, https://www.vera.org/downloads/publications/a-look-inside-the-new-york-city-correction-budget.pdf.

107 In 2022, nineteen people died at Rikers Island. Erica Bryant, "19 People Have Died from New York City Jails in 2022," Vera Institute of Justice, December 12, 2022, https://www.vera.org/news/nyc-jail-deaths-2022#:~:text=Image%20courtesy%20of%20the%20%23HALTsolitary,Kross%20Center%20on%20Rikers%20Island.

108 See the *Washington Post*'s "Fatal Force" database: https://www.washingtonpost.com/graphics/investigations/police-shootings-database.

109 See George L. Kelling and James Q. Wilson, "Broken Windows: The Police and Neighborhood Safety," *Atlantic*. https://www.theatlantic.com/magazine/archive/1982/03/broken-windows/304465/. See Bernard E. Harcourt, *Illusion of Order: The False Promise of Broken Windows Policing* (Cambridge, MA: Harvard University Press, 2004); and Randall G. Shelden, "Assessing Broken Windows: A Brief

Critique," Center on Juvenile and Criminal Justice, https://www.cjcj. org/media/import/documents/broken.pdf.

110 Derrick A. Bell, "Who's Afraid of Critical Race Theory?," *University of Illinois Law Review* 1995, no. 4 (1995): 893–910.

111 See Larry Buchana, Quoctrung Bul, and Jugal K. Patel, "Black Lives Matter May Be the Largest Movement in U.S. History," *New York Times,* July 3, 2020, https://www.nytimes.com/interactive/2020/07/03/us/george-floyd-protests-crowd-size.html.

112 See "New York Police Department Disciplinary Data," New York Civil Liberties Union, https://www.nyclu.org/en/campaigns/nypd-discipline-numbers.

113 See Jordan Hoffman, "Eric Adams Wants to End Drill Rap Now That He Knows What It Is," *Vanity Fair,* February 12, 2022, https://www.vanityfair.com/style/2022/02/eric-adams-wants-to-end-drill-rap-now-that-he-knows-what-it-is.

114 See "Citywide Crime Statistics," NYPD, https://www.nyc.gov/site/nypd/stats/crime-statistics/citywide-crime-stats.page.

115 See Nick Pinto, "America's Crisis Daddy Andrew Cuomo Exploits Coronavirus Panic to Push Bail Reform Rollback in New York," *Intercept,* March 25, 2022, https://theintercept.com/2020/03/25/coronavirus-andrew-cuomo-new-york-bail-reform.

CHAPTER 5

116 At the time of our interview, Professor Ilan was a senior lecturer at City, University of London.

117 See Jonathan Ilan, *Understanding Street Culture: Poverty, Crime, Youth, and Cool* (New York: Palgrave, 2015).

118 See Jonathan Ilan, "Digital Street Culture Decoded: Why Criminalizing Drill Music is Street Illiterate and Counterproductive," *British Journal of Criminology* 60, no. 4 (July 2020): 994–1013, https://doi:10.1093/bjc/azz086.

119 Kat Devlin et al., "Outside U.S., Floyd's Killing and Protests Sparked Discussion on Legislators' Twitter Accounts," Pew Research Center, August 4, 2020, https://www.pewresearch.org/fact-tank/2020/08/04/outside-u-s-floyds-killing-and-protests-sparked-discussion-on-legislators-twitter-accounts.

120 See May Bulman, "Rashan Charles: Man Dies after Being Chased and Arrested by London Police, Sparking Independent Investigation," *Independent,* July 23, 2017, https://www.independent.co.uk/news/uk/home-news/rashan-charles-rashman-rash-man-dies-dead-london-police-dalston-chase-ipcc-met-video-cctv-swallowed-a7855376.html; Lizzie Dearden, "Edson Da Costa: Young Father Restrained by Police Died by 'Misadventure' after Putting Drugs in Mouth, Inquest Finds," *Independent,* June 7, 2019, https://www.independent.co.uk/news/uk/

crime/edson-da-costa-death-inquest-police-restraint-drugs-black-men-a8948366.html.

121 See Jason Strother, "America's BLM Protests Find Solidarity in South Korea," *World*, June 8, 2020, https://theworld.org/stories/2020-06-08/america-s-blm-protests-find-solidarity-south-korea.

122 See Martin Farrer, "Who Was Edward Colston and Why Was His Bristol Statue Toppled?," *Guardian*, June 8, 2020, https://www.theguardian.com/uk-news/2020/jun/08/who-was-edward-colston-and-why-was-his-bristol-statue-toppled-slave-trader-black-lives-matter-protests.

123 See Amit Chaudhuri, "The Real Meaning of Rhodes Must Fall," *Guardian*, March 16, 2016, https://www.theguardian.com/uk-news/2016/mar/16/the-real-meaning-of-rhodes-must-fall.

124 See Human Rights Watch, *Sex Workers at Risk: Condoms as Evidence of Prostitution in Four US Cities*, 2012, https://www.hrw.org/report/2012/07/19/sex-workers-risk/condoms-evidence-prostitution-four-us-cities.

125 "Drill" is slang for shooting or stabbing.

126 See Forrest Stuart, *Ballad of the Bullet: Gangs, Drill Music, and the Power of Online Infamy* (Princeton, NJ: Princeton University Press, 2021).

127 See Chief Keef, "Don't Like," YouTube, March 12, 2012, https://www.youtube.com/watch?v=2WcRXJ4piHg&ab_channel=DGainz.

128 This is also the title of rap artist 50 Cent's debut album and has become a colloquial phrase within hip hop culture.

129 Ilan, "Digital Street Culture Decoded."

130 Paul Gilroy, *The Black Atlantic: Modernity and Double-Consciousness* (Cambridge, MA: Harvard University Press, 1993).

131 Eleni Dimou and Jonathan Ilan, "Taking Pleasure Seriously: The Political Significance of Subcultural Practice," *Journal of Youth Studies* 21, no. 1 (2018): 1–18, https://doi.org/10.1080/13676261.2017.1340635.

132 See Émile Durkheim, *The Division of Labor in Society* (New York: Free Press, 2014).

133 See Paul Lewis et al., "Student Protest over Fees Turn Violent," *Guardian*, November 10, 2010, https://www.theguardian.com/education/2010/nov/10/student-protest-fees-violent.

134 CrookedMC, "N.W.A. on Arsenio Hall," (September 1990), *YouTube*, https://www.youtube.com/watch?v=rPJjb5JIMEU&t=415s&ab_channel=CrookedMC.

135 See David Lammy, *The Lammy Review: An Independent Review into the Treatment of, and Outcomes for, Black, Asian and Minority Ethnic individuals in the Criminal Justice System*, https://assets.publishing.service.gov.uk/government/uploads/system/uploads/attachment_data/file/643001/lammy-review-final-report.pdf.

136 See Julia Angwin et al., "Machine Bias," *ProPublica*, May 23, 2016, https://www.propublica.org/article/machine-bias-risk-assessments-in-

criminal-sentencing. See Aaron Sankin and Surya Mattu, "Predictive Policing Software Terrible at Predicting Crimes," *The Markup*, October 2, 2023, https://themarkup.org/prediction-bias/2023/10/02/predictive-policing-software-terrible-at-predicting-crimes

137   See Jock Young, *The Criminological Imagination* (Cambridge, UK: Polity, 2011).

138   See Angela Davis, *Abolition Democracy: Beyond Empire, Prisons, and Torture* (New York: Seven Stories, 2005).

139   A saying often attributed to the eighteenth-century writer and philosopher Voltaire.

CHAPTER 6

140   For more in-depth information on MOVE and supporters of MOVE, see Mike Africa Jr., *40 Years a Prisoner* (HBOMax, 2020); Marc Evans, *In Prison My Whole Life* (Netflix, 2008); J. Patrick O'Connor, *The Framing of Mumia Abu-Jamal* (Chicago: Chicago Review Press, 2008); Mumia Abu-Jamal, *Jailhouse Lawyers: Prisoners Defending Prisoners v. the USA* (San Francisco: City Lights 2009); Richard Kent Evans, *MOVE: An American Religion* (New York: Oxford University Press, 2020).

141   See Emma Whitford, "Man Who Filmed Eric Garner's Murder Begins 4-Year Prison Sentence Today," *Gothamist*, October 3, 2016, https://gothamist.com/news/man-who-filmed-eric-garners-murder-begins-4-year-prison-sentence-today.

142   Mumia Abu-Jamal has been incarcerated since December 1981, stemming from a shooting that left a Philadelphia police officer dead. Prior to his incarceration, Mumia was a member of the Black Panther Party as a teenager and an investigative journalist in the city of Philadelphia. One of the most recognizable political prisoners in American history, Mumia has authored or coauthored over a dozen books. He spent the first thirty years of his incarceration on death row before being resentenced in 2011 to life imprisonment without the possibility of parole. For more information on the Free Mumia movement, see: https://freemumia.com and https://bringmumiahome.com.

143   This lighthearted comment alludes not that Debbie and Mike are no longer championing human, animal, and environmental rights but rather to a shift in their strategy and forms of engagement.

144   See Justin Heinze, "Graterford Prison Water System Has Toxin Made Famous by Erin Brockovich, Study Says," *Patch*, September 21, 2016, https://patch.com/pennsylvania/limerick/graterford-prison-water-system-has-toxin-made-famous-erin-brockovich-study.

145   See Matt Breen, "Bernard Hopkins' Hall of Fame Career Started with a Visit in Prison from a Boxing Ref Named Rudy Battle," *Philadelphia Inquirer*, July 22, 2022, https://www.inquirer.com/sports/bernard-hopkins-rudy-battle-boxing-hall-of-fame-20220722.html.

146 I was thirty-five years old at time of interview, in December 2021.

147 Merle Africa, the first MOVE 9 member to pass on, died in 1998 while incarcerated.

148 Mike is referring to "race riots" in Tulsa, Oklahoma, in 1921 and in Rosewood, Florida, in 1923, in which Black communities in these areas were attacked by unprovoked White mobs. For more, see Scott Ellsworth, *Death in a Promised Land: The Tulsa Race Riot of 1921* (Baton Rouge: Louisiana State University Press, 1992); and Edward González-Tennat, *The Rosewood Massacre: An Archeology and History of Intersectional Violence* (Gainesville: University Press of Florida, 2019).

149 See May Day Space: https://maydayspace.org/. A community center and organizing hub for groups, residents, artists, and activists to build a better world.

150 See "Some Texas Schools May Call Slavery 'Involuntary Relocation,'" *AP News*, June 30, 2022, https://apnews.com/article/texas-education-slavery-fort-worth-government-and-politics-b081853905b9c871a90dafc918a17143.

151 See Samantha Michaels, "Pennsylvania Replaced Prison Mail with Photocopies. Inmates and Their Families Are Heartbroken," *Mother Jones*, December 13, 2018, https://www.motherjones.com/crime-justice/2018/12/pennsylvania-replaced-prison-mail-with-photocopies-inmates-and-their-families-are-heartbroken.

152 Pennsylvania uses JPay, a private information technology and financial provider in the US prison system. For more on its fees, see PA JPay FAQ sheet: https://www.cor.pa.gov/Inmates/Documents/JPAY%20FAQ.pdf

153 Pennsylvania Department of Corrections uses Connect Network. See https://www.cor.pa.gov/family-and-friends/Pages/Inmate-E-Mail.aspx.

154 See Alondra Nelson, *Body and Soul: The Black Panther Party and the Fight against Medical Discrimination* (Minneapolis, MN: University of Minnesota Press, 2013). See Suzanne Cope, *Power Hunter· Women of the Black Panther Party and Freedom Summer and Their Fight to Feed a Movement* (Chicago, IL: Lawerence Hill Books, 2021).

155 See Alice Speri, "A Chokehold Didn't Kill Eric Garner, Your Disrespect for the NYPD Did," *Intercept*, August 6, 2014, https://www.vice.com/en/article/59a4en/a-chokehold-didnt-kill-eric-garner-your-disrespect-for-the-nypd-did.

156 Delbert Africa was infamously beaten by Philadelphia police on August 8, 1978, after he surrendered, shirtless, with his arms raised.

157 See Khrysgiana Pineda, "Controversial Statue of Former Philadelphia Mayor Frank Rizzo Removed after George Floyd Protests," *USA Today*, June 3, 2020, https://www.usatoday.com/story/news/nation/2020/06/03/frank-rizzo-statue-philadelphia-city-hall-removed/3134229001/.

158 See John Ismay, "35 Years After MOVE Bombing That Killed 11, Philadelphia Apologizes," *New York Times*, November 13, 2020, https://

www.nytimes.com/2020/11/13/us/philadelphia-bombing-apology-move.html#:~:text=The%20Philadelphia%20City%20Council%20 this,people%20and%20destroyed%2061%20homes.

159 Baartman, a South African Black woman, was trotted around Europe in the early 19th century and her remains put on display at various French museums until the late 20th century. See Sadiah Qureshi, "Displaying Sara Baartman, the 'Hottentot Venus,'" *History of Science* 42, no. 2 (2004): 233–57, https://doi.org/10.1177/007327530404200204.

CHAPTER 7

160 See Action Center on Race and the Economy, which fights for racial and economic justice by exposing and challenging financial institutions and political actors who profit at the expense of communities of color: https://acrecampaigns.org/

161 For details on the AfroSocialists and Socialists of Color Caucus of the Democratic Socialists of America, see the DSA website: https://www. dsausa.org/working-groups/afrosocialists-and-socialists-of-color-caucus.

162 See Jasson Perez, interviewed by brian bean, "The Black Abolitionist Network," *Rampant*, July 10, 2020, https://rampantmag.com/2020/07/ the-black-abolitionist-network.

163 See Sean Campbell, "Black Lives Matter Secretly Bought a $6 Million House. Allies and Critics Alike Have Questioned Where the Organization's Money Has Gone," *New York Magazine*, April 4, 2022, https://nymag.com/intelligencer/2022/04/black-lives-matter-6-million-dollar-house.html.

164 See Saul Alinsky, *Rules for Radicals: A Practical Primer for Realistic Radicals* (New York: Vintage, 1989 [1971]).

165 Alleen Brown, "'We Don't Have Time to Wait': Minneapolis Anti–Police Brutality Organizer Kandace Montgomery on Defunding the Police," *Intercept*, June 5, 2020, https://theintercept.com/2020/06/05/ defund-the-police-minneapolis-black-visions-collective.

166 See Maya King, "How 'Defund the Police' Went from Moonshot to Mainstream," *Politico*, June 17, 2020, https://www.politico.com/states/ new-york/city-hall/story/2020/06/17/how-defund-the-police-went-from-moonshot-to-mainstream-1293451#:~:text=One%20of%20 them%2C%20the%20women,headline%20on%20the%20petition%20 read.

167 For a discussion of the concept of nonreformist reform, see Mark Engler and Paul Angler, "André Gorz's Non-Reformist Reforms Show How We Can Transform the World Today," *Jacobin*, July 22, 2021, https:// jacobin.com/2021/07/andre-gorz-non-reformist-reforms-revolution-political-theory.

168 *Jacobin* magazine is a self-described "leading voice of the American

left, offering socialist perspectives on politics, economics, and culture":
https://jacobin.com.

169 Jasson Perez et al., *21st Century Policing: The RISE and REACH of
Surveillance Technology* (Chicago: ACRE and Community Resource
Hub, April 19, 2021), https://acrecampaigns.org/wp-content/
uploads/2021/03/acre-21stcenturypolicing-r4-web.pdf.

170 For more on "e-incarceration," see Michelle Alexander, "The Newest
Jim Crow," *New York Times*, November 8, 2018, https://www.nytimes.
com/2018/11/08/opinion/sunday/criminal-justice-reforms-race-
technology.html.

171 See Herbert H. Haines, "Black Radicalization and the Funding of Civil
Rights: 1957–1970," *Social Problems* 32, no. 1 (1984–85): 31–43.

172 See John Clegg and Adaner Usmani, "The Economic Origins of Mass
Incarceration," *Catalyst* 3, no. 3 (Fall 2019): 9–53, https://catalyst-
journal.com/2019/12/the-economic-origins-of-mass-incarceration.

173 See Peter Ikeler and Calvin John Smiley, "The Racial Economics
of Mass Incarceration," *Spectre* 1, no. 2 (Fall 2020): 78–99, https://
spectrejournal.com/the-racial-economics-of-mass-incarceration/.

174 See John Jay College of Criminal Justice Research and Evaluation
Center Cure Violence Glossary: https://johnjayrec.nyc/2015/04/17/
cvglossary/. Credible messengers can relate to the population because
they are deemed "credible" as being part of that community to curb
violence. Violence Interrupters are responsible for gauging the pulse of
a community to reduce violence and mediate conflict.

175 The Cabrini-Green Homes were part of Chicago Housing Authority
(1942–2011).

176 See Block Clubs are groups of people who organize to improve the
quality of life in neighborhoods: https://home.chicagopolice.org/
community-policing-group/special-projects/block-clubs/

177 See Civil Liberties Defense Center, "De-Arresting: Important Legal
Information for Street Actions," September 9, 2022, https://cldc.org/de-
arresting.

178 See Frances Fox Piven, *Poor People's Movements: Why They Succeed,
How They Fail* (New York: Vintage, 1978).

179 Joe Biden, "Remarks of President Joe Biden – State of the Union
Address as Prepared for Delivery," The White House, March
1, 2022, https://www.whitehouse.gov/briefing-room/speeches-
remarks/2022/03/01/remarks-of-president-joe-biden-state-of-the-
union-address-as-delivered/.

CONCLUSION

180 Dylan Rodriguez, "Abolition as Praxis of Human Being: A Foreword,"
Harvard Law Review 132, no. 6 (April 2019): 1575–1612.

181 Rodríguez, "Abolition as Praxis," 1610.

182 Romare Bearden, *The Block* (New York: Metropolitan Museum of Art, 1971), https://www.metmuseum.org/art/collection/search/481891.

183 Jeffrey Fagan, Valier West, and Jan Holland, "Reciprocal Effects of Crime and Incarceration in New York City Neighborhoods," *Fordham Urban Law Journal* 30, no. 5 (2002): 1550–62.

184 Jane Jacobs, *The Death and Life of Great American Cities* (New York: Vintage, 1961).

185 Ailey, Alvin, James Baldwin, Romare Bearden, and Albert Murray. "'To Hear Another Language." *Callaloo* 24, no. 2 (2001): 656-677.

186 Mariame Kaba, *We Do This 'Til We Free Us: Abolitionist Organizing and Transforming Justice* (Chicago: Haymarket, 2021).

Index